Phil Hellmuth
presents

Read'Em
and
Reap

Phil Hellmuth
presents
Read'Em and Reap

A Career FBI Agent's Guide
to Decoding Poker Tells

Joe Navarro
with
Marvin Karlins, Ph.D.

An Imprint of HarperCollinsPublishers

HarperCollins books may be purchased for educational, business, or sales promotional use. For information, please write: Special Markets Department, HarperCollins Publishers, Inc., 10 East 53rd Street, New York, NY 10022.

FIRST EDITION

Library of Congress Cataloging-in-Publication Data is available upon request.

ISBN-10: 0-06-119859-5
ISBN-13: 978-0-06-119859-5

07 08 09 10 WBC/RRD 10 9 8 7 6 5

To my daughter Stephanie

Acknowledgments

One of the joys in writing a book is meeting and working with very talented and dedicated individuals. Our heartfelt appreciation goes to Matthew Benjamin, our editor at HarperCollins, who gave us unwavering support and valuable advice during all phases of this project. We are grateful to senior production editor Amy Vreeland and copy editor Jim Gullickson for catching our writing errors and making the text eminently more readable. Special recognition is also merited by the two gentlemen who put this whole project together: Jeff Goldenberg and Brandon Rosen at Post Oak Productions. We would also like to acknowledge the contributions of Jim Lewis (Phil's manager), Brian Balsbaugh, (Phil's agent), Andrew Feldman (ESPN Poker Club), and professional poker champions John Bonetti, T. J. Cloutier, Annie Duke, and Antonio Esfandiari. The cover photograph was provided by Joe Coomber, while the pictures inside the book were taken by Sonny Sensor (www.sonnyphoto.com). Paul Lord and his team at the Caesars Palace Poker Room in Las Vegas were very helpful, as were the staff from the Seminole Hard Rock Hotel & Casino in Tampa: John Fontana, president; Russ Christianson, Casino vice president; Mary Lynn Babetski, advertising manager; Gary Bitner, public relations representative; and the poker room staff. We would also like to recognize the individuals who appeared in the various pictures throughout the book: Soudara "Noi" Phrathep (casino dealer) and players Don Delitz, Amber Karlins, Robert Mercado, and Richard Ollis. To each of you, please accept our gratitude for all your efforts in our behalf. We couldn't have completed this project without you!

Personal thanks go out to my family and to my friends, especially Dr. Juan Ling, M.D., for his friendship over the years, which directly contributed to my involvement in this project. My gratitude also goes out to Dr. David Givens, Ph.D., Marc Reeser, Elizabeth Barron, and Dr. Joyce Jackiewicz, Psy.D., for their valued insight.

Finally, I want to thank the man who gave life to my words, Dr. Marvin Karlins. He has blessed me with his friendship, which turned hard work into pleasure.

Contents

Foreword

Tells Make All the Difference!

by Phil Hellmuth Jr.
Ten-time World Champion of Poker

When I sit down at a poker table, I play a game within the game: I try to guess exactly what two cards my opponent has in the hole. I can usually narrow it down to a very few possibilities, and on occasion I have ventured a guess out loud when I felt confident about it. Boy, did I freak the other players out when I would guess my main opponent's Q-Q and he would then flip his Q-Q faceup and say, "How in the world does he do that?"

How in the world *do* I do it? Primarily through *reading people,* observing and deciphering their *tells,* the nonverbal behaviors that reveal the strength of the cards they're holding. It is amazing how many poker players, even some world-class professionals, are unaware that they're offering tells that render their hands transparent. These individuals might just as well turn their cards faceup and give their money away.

I clearly remember noticing a key tell by my well-known opponent in one World Series of Poker (WSOP) tournament that

I wound up winning in 1997. Every time this opponent was going to fold his hand, he would put his chips halfway into the pot before it was his turn to act. So whenever I was in a pot with him and he was contemplating my move, he would push his chips halfway into the pot if he was weak. In one hand, the flop was A-9-8, and I checked with my 7-5. He bet out $14,000, and I began to think about what I wanted to do. With $65,000 left in chips, it was an obvious fold situation with my belly buster (inside straight draw). But suddenly, he pushed his chips halfway into the pot, and I knew I should move all-in! I pushed, he folded, and I went on to win my fifth WSOP bracelet.

In another tournament, at the 2001 WSOP, with two tables remaining, I noticed that whenever the player sitting to my right raised, he would lean back in his chair when he was weak. Conversely, he would lean forward when he was strong. Every time he leaned forward, I folded. Every time he leaned back, I pounced (I reraised and he folded). This allowed me to more than double up my chips with absolutely nothing in my hand, risk free. Just one tell on one opponent had allowed me to double my stack!

It is experiences like these, over the years, that have led me to formulate Hellmuth's "Tournament Poker 70-30 Rule": success in the game is 70 percent reading people and only 30 percent reading the cards (understanding the mathematical and technical aspects of the game). Tells *do* make all the difference!

Which brings me to Joe Navarro, a man who uses tells so successfully that he has earned the nickname "the Human Lie Detector." Joe first came to my attention when fellow professional Annie Duke mentioned his name. She had been on a television program with him and was impressed with his ability to read people and determine if they were being deceptive or telling the truth. About a year later, the folks behind Camp Hellmuth, my poker fantasy camp (which has now merged with the WSOP Academy), told me they had hired Joe to give a seminar on tells for the camp participants. Little did I know at the time that he would receive better marks and higher praise from the campers for his session than for any other session offered, including mine! In fact, T. J. Cloutier and I both took three pages of notes during Joe's one-hour presentation, which clearly demonstrated the importance we attached to what we were hearing. Later, we both expressed our amazement that we had taken *any* notes at all, much less three pages worth, since neither of us had ever taken notes at any previous poker seminars.

I was so impressed with Joe that I invited him to be part of the iAmplify.com project, where he provides 5-to-20-minute "blasts" in MP3 and MP4 formats for iPods and cell phones about nonverbal tells. Joe, you see, has been studying and using these nonverbal behaviors to detect deception and solve cases involving criminals and international terrorists during a distinguished 25-year career as a special agent with the FBI. His information is steeped in cutting-edge science, the kind that can help poker players *and* the U.S. government detect and decipher what their opponents are up to.

Joe also does individual consulting with top poker players throughout the world. In these one-on-one sessions, he will let players know what tells they project, but he will not reveal these tells to their competitors. I was one of the beneficiaries of this consulting opportunity. It turns out that Joe had watched me play in a no-limit Hold'em tournament on television and noted that I had a glaring tell. Every time I bluffed, I would wrap my arms around my body in a kind of reassuring hug. The bad news was that the other players at the table picked up on my nonverbal tell and took me to the cleaners. That little gesture ended up costing me a quarter of a million dollars. The good news is that Joe informed me of the tell, and my hugging days are now over!

In this book, Joe presents you with priceless scientific information on tells, the kind that can make the difference between winning and losing at the poker table. This information has never been presented before, except at the Camp Hellmuth seminars. *It takes poker to a new level and gives players a choice: they can either open the book and read it or become an open book that others can read.*

If T. J. Cloutier and I can find enough valuable information in Joe's material to take three pages of notes at his seminar, imagine what you'll get out of this book. The information you need to better read people by observing their tells and, conversely, to hide your own tells is revealed in these pages. If you're really astute, perhaps you can learn to give off false tells of strength when you're actually weak, and of weakness when you're actually strong. Let the games begin!

Let me end with this: I'll wager that this book pays for itself the very first time you sit down at the poker table. Good luck.

Preface

Meet the Man Who Will Change the Face of Poker and Your Poker Face

by Marvin Karlins, Ph.D.

April 17, 1971. Everything happened so quickly that warm spring day in Hialeah, Florida. Two knife-wielding thieves bolted from the back of Richard's Department Store as the manager cried out for help. They ran toward the front of the building, knowing that beyond the doorway they could disappear into the crowded street outside. An employee, a 17-year-old high school senior, moved to intercept them, blocking their escape route. The confrontation was short and violent. In a matter of seconds, the young man disabled one assailant and tripped the other, even as he himself fell to the ground, stabbed so severely that it took 180 stitches to close his wound. His quick action led to the apprehension of both assailants. A short time later, this youngster received a personal letter from the president of the United States commending him for his heroism in foiling the robbery.

▪ ▪ ▪ ▪ ▪

July 9, 1987. It was an extremely serious case of espionage: an American soldier had attempted to obtain very sensitive, top secret materials; materials that, by the definition of the attorney general, would do irrevocable, grievous harm to the United States and its allies. As the man was interrogated, investigators became convinced that he was not acting alone. While he was willing to discuss his involvement in the case, he refused to implicate his coconspirators. Attempts to appeal to his sense of patriotism and concern for the millions of people he was placing in harm's way got no response. Things were at an impasse. A Special Agent was brought in, a man who had an idea for getting the information so urgently needed. First, a list of all possible coconspirators was compiled. It included the names of 32 men who had access to the top secret materials. Then each name was placed on a three-by-five card. Finally, the soldier was shown all the cards, one at a time, and asked to tell, in general terms, what he knew about each individual. The Special Agent wasn't concerned with the soldier's answers; rather, he was watching his face. When the man saw two names in particular, his eyebrows lifted a little bit and then the pupils of his eyes constricted. The Special Agent, an expert in reading "body language," knew that the arching of the eyebrow signified recognition and the pupillary constriction indicated a threat response. It was all he needed to know. He gathered up the cards and left. The next day, he came back with two pictures of the men the soldier had reacted to and said, "Tell me about this one and this one . . ." The soldier's eyes got as wide as saucers. "How did you know?" he asked in astonishment. The Special Agent said, "Do you really think you're the only one who's cooperating with me?" At that point the soldier said, "Those sons of bitches!" and proceeded to spill his guts. All three men were convicted of espionage.

▮ ▮ ▮ ▮ ▮

October 14, 2005. The observer shifted slightly in his chair to get a better view of the TV monitors and stared intently at the World Poker Tour (WPT) broadcast on the high-definition screen. A few minutes later, he retrieved a DVD of final-table action at the World Series of Poker and replayed one particular hand three times in succession. He reached for a pen and jotted down his observations on a legal pad atop his desk.

Outside the viewing room, the observer was approached by a writer. "Were you able to spot any tells?" the writer asked.

The observer nodded affirmatively. "The players I studied all gave off nonverbal cues that could be used to determine the strength of their hand and/or if they intended to bet."

The writer was astonished. "But you were watching *professionals.* I thought only amateur players were guilty of giving off tells."

"Not true," the observer insisted. "I've been able to spot tells in every major tournament player I've studied."

"Guys like, say, Doyle Brunson?"

"Yes."

"Phil Ivey?"

"Him, too."

"Phil Hellmuth?"

"Go back and read the foreword to this book," the observer quipped.

"What about Chris Ferguson?"

"Chris was difficult to read," the observer admitted, "but in the end I detected a major tell."

The writer rubbed at his chin with his right hand. "That's

extremely useful information, I'm sure you could sell it for a lot of money."

"I could," the observer agreed, "but I won't because that would be unethical."

■ ■ ■ ■ ■

Welcome to the world of Joe Navarro, teenage hero, recently retired counterintelligence and counterterrorism special agent with the FBI, and consultant to professional and would-be professional poker players worldwide.

Joe is one of the good guys. He's soft-spoken, intelligent, thoughtful, and gracious . . . a kind of Joe Friday with a personality. He's the type of person you'd be proud to have in your home, the kind of guest you'd love to invite over so you could sit across from him and exchange views at the dinner table.

Just *don't* invite him to sit across from you at the poker table . . . at least until you read this book, otherwise you could be on the fast track to financial ruin. Joe, it turns out, has spent his entire career studying, refining, and applying the science of nonverbal behavior to decipher what you are thinking, how you intend to act, and whether your pronouncements are true or false. This is *not* good news for his poker opponents, who, under his careful scrutiny, usually give off more than enough nonverbal "tells" to make their cards *and* their moves basically transparent.

When I first met Joe I asked him, "How does a man who spent a quarter century busting bad guys for the FBI ever get involved with a bunch of poker players in the first place?" It seemed like a strange combination.

"It happened quite by accident," he explained. "In 2004, the Discovery Channel asked me to participate in a show called *More Than Human*. The idea of the program was to see if people were superior to machines when it came to detecting whether someone was lying or telling the truth. The television people who developed the story line selected three individuals whose occupations involved detecting lies: myself, a psychic by the name of Dr. Louis Turi, and Annie Duke, a world-champion poker player. We were pitted against three machines designed to accomplish the same objective: a polygraph, a voice stress analyzer, and a pupil dilation apparatus. The challenge was to see who could best tell if an actor was lying or telling the truth based on twenty-five different verbal statements he made. It turned out that Dr. Turi was less than fifty percent accurate, while Annie and I both detected the correct answer eighteen out of twenty-five times—which, by the way, beat two out of the three machines for accuracy."

"Were you surprised that Annie did so well?" I asked.

"That was the interesting thing," Joe exclaimed. "As we were being tested on our ability to detect deception, I noticed that Annie looked for a lot of the same things I was looking for. She didn't use the same names I used for what she saw, but her ability to read people was extremely accurate. Naturally, we talked about it. Annie is an extremely delightful, funny, outgoing person . . . very congenial and full of stories. Those who have seen her play poker on television, where she's all business, would probably be shocked to learn of her gregarious nature."

I mentioned that Annie had written an article in *Bluff* magazine in which she claimed that meeting Joe "was a turning point in my No Limit Hold'em game" and that when he provided her with additional information on his work in nonverbal tells "my poker game took a jump to the next level."

Joe smiled and returned the compliment: "Meeting Annie Duke was a turning point for me as well; she was the one who turned me on to poker. It was through our conversations that I realized the skills I had used to 'read people' and uncover deception in my twenty-five years with the FBI were also applicable at the poker table. Thanks to Annie, I had a new venue where I could study human behavior and, at the same time, teach poker players how to achieve greater success by recognizing their opponents tells while concealing their own at the same time."

Taking Poker Tells to the Next Level

After interviewing Joe and attending his seminars, I firmly believe the material in this book will revolutionize our understanding of nonverbal behavior at the tables. I say this as a trained psychologist who got involved with writing this book because I was excited by Joe's pioneering success in harnessing *scientific* knowledge to play poker more effectively. This is the first book on poker tells to be based on scientific fact rather than personal opinion. It is also the first book that draws on knowledge of the human brain to develop and create powerful playing tactics that have never been revealed before.

As a participant in major poker tournaments, I am also impressed with Joe's work on a personal level. By following his recommendations, I have become a better player, a more formidable opponent. So will you. Joe's insights will allow you to detect and decipher a whole new set of heretofore unknown tells, many so subtle and innocuous that it is only through your new knowledge that you will be able to spot them in others, while taking steps to eliminate these tells in your own game.

Much of what Joe will be sharing with you in this book was

not even recognized 15 years ago. It is only through recent advances in brain-scan technology and neural imaging that scientists have been able to establish the validity of the behaviors Joe will be describing. Drawing from the latest discoveries in psychology, neurobiology, medicine, sociology, criminology, communication studies, and anthropology—plus his 25 years of practical experience using nonverbal behavior in his work as an FBI Special Agent—Joe will help you determine if that big raiser across the table truly has the nuts or is bluffing. Along the way, you'll also discover that the tells you're trained to identify at the poker table can also serve you well in *all* your personal interactions, whether it be dating, dealing with your children, conducting or giving a good interview, buying a car, or even deciding when to ask your boss for a raise.

Best of all, the information in this book can be used *throughout* each poker session. In this sense, Navarro's insights are better than pocket aces: like "pocket rockets," they give the player a powerful edge, but whereas pocket aces show up only once every 221 hands, the Navarro insights can be used on every hand dealt!

We know Joe's recommendations work: testimonials by world poker champions attest to that; so do Camp Hellmuth participants who report using Navarro's strategy to win back their seminar costs and much more in just a few short hours of play at the tables.

So get ready to enter the brave new world of poker. Your ticket of admission is a careful reading of the chapters that follow, plus the commitment to invest serious time and effort in learning and applying Joe's teachings at the table. I believe you will find your efforts well spent. Remember, there will be literally millions of players who *haven't* yet read this book or are unwill-

ing to devote the effort necessary to use what they've learned to
gain significant benefits. That gives you a tremendous edge. Take
full measure of your advantage, and as you observe your opponents across the table, you'll be able to . . .

"Read 'em and reap!"

You can bet on it.

Chapter 1

How to Become a Serious Threat at the Poker Table

I presume you want to do your best when you sit down at a poker table. No matter what your level, be it amateur or professional, beginner or seasoned veteran, I realize you've spent your money on this book to improve your game. I, in turn, want you to walk away knowing that you can use what you've learned to achieve that objective.

I'm going to treat you just like the FBI special agents I train. It's a no-nonsense approach. I take my assignments seriously because I know that what I'm teaching can make the difference between life and death in an agent's work. For you poker enthusiasts, the consequences of not learning and using what I'm presenting will not get you killed, but it can be deleterious to your financial well-being. So, let's see what we can do to keep your bankroll healthy.

A Lesson from Medical School

The first-year medical students filed into the amphitheater for their final class in Dr. Patel's human physiology course. Dr. Patel was the oldest professor at the university with a reputation as a strict disciplinarian, so when he arrived with his well-worn medical bag grasped firmly in his right hand, not a sound was heard in the oval-shaped room.

Dr. Patel stepped up to the speaker's platform, extracted a beaker of yellow fluid from his bag, and placed it on the lectern in front of him. "I have an issue I want to discuss with you today," he began, a hint of anger in his voice. "I've heard a rumor around here that some of you think we're working you too hard: that the assignments are too difficult, the hours too long." The doctor paused and studied the faces of the students who sat in the tiered seats above him. "Well, let me tell you something," he said sternly. "You don't know how easy you have it! When *I* was in medical school, we worked just as long and hard as you do, plus we didn't have the plush facilities and modern laboratories you all take for granted. For instance," he asked the class, "how do you test for diabetes?"

A female student spoke from the third row. "Well, you can collect a urine specimen and send it to the lab for analysis."

"OK," Dr. Patel replied. "And then what?"

The woman shifted in her seat. "You get the lab report back and make a treatment decision based on the results."

"Exactly," exclaimed the doctor. "Well, in my day we didn't have all those fancy laboratories and diagnostic clinics. Lots of times we had to run the tests ourselves, with no help from anyone else. For example, you know how *I* had to test for diabetes?"

The woman shook her head and said "no."

"I'll tell you how: *taste*."

This time the woman shook her head in disbelief.

"That's right," the doctor asserted. "If the sample was sweet, well, that patient had a problem." He picked up the beaker full of yellow fluid. "This is a urine specimen from the lab. And you know what? I've never lost my diagnostic skills." Having said that, the students saw him dip his finger into the urine and lick it.

"That's *gross*," the medical student declared, her facial expression remindful of someone who had just swallowed raw lemon juice. A chorus of similar reactions throughout the room indicated her revulsion was not unique.

"Hey, at least it's not diabetes," the doctor declared, wiping his hand on a handkerchief he pulled from his lab coat. That didn't seem to ease the students' unrest over witnessing the "diagnosis." They kept speaking to each other in whispered tones until Dr. Patel finally ordered them to be still.

"Now, I suppose some of you are wondering why I concocted this little demonstration," he continued, placing the beaker back on the podium. "There are two reasons, actually. The first is to remind you that medical school has never been easy, and if you can't handle the pressure maybe this is a good time to get out. Now, as a lasting reminder of how difficult medical education is, I want each of you to come up here and do exactly as I did." The doctor tapped on the beaker full or urine. "I want you to get a 'taste' of how difficult medical school can really be."

Nobody left their seat.

"C'mon now, this is no time to be shy."

Not a person moved.

"How about a little gentle persuasion, then," the doctor suggested. "You need to pass this course to continue your studies . . . so if you *don't* do as I say, I'm going to fail you right out of med school."

That seemed to work. Reluctantly, slowly, and with obvious dismay the students approached the podium, dipped their fingers into the beaker, tasted the urine, and beat a hasty retreat to the bathroom before returning to their seats.

Once everyone returned to the classroom, the doctor began speaking again. "As important as the first reason was for this little demonstration, the second reason is even more critical." Taking a moment to place the beaker back in his medical bag, Dr. Patel paused to give added emphasis to his words.

"The second reason for the urine demonstration is to teach you the importance of *observation* in your work as doctors. Someday you may be examining a patient who is telling you one thing, while their body language is telling you something else. If you are observing them closely, you might pick up on this discrepancy and make a more informed, accurate diagnosis.

"Just *how* important is observation?" Dr. Patel allowed a hint of a smile to punctuate his final words. "Well, if you had been watching me closely, you would have noticed I dipped my index finger into the urine, but I licked my middle finger!"

Conscientious Observation: The Foundation of Our Poker Strategy

I suspect that Dr. Patel is a fictitious character and the "medical school story" another example of an urban myth. Nevertheless, I included the tale because it makes an important point. If he practiced what he preached, Dr. Patel would be a formidable force at the poker table. This is because observation—conscientious (effortful) observation—is absolutely essential to reading people and detecting their tells successfully.

The problem is that most people spend their lives *looking* but not truly *seeing*; that is, they view their surroundings with the minimal amount of observational effort to get by. Such people are oblivious to subtle changes in their world. They would be unlikely to perceive the rich tapestry of details that surround them, let alone ever distinguishing between an index or middle finger being dipped in urine . . . or a hand gesture across a poker table that indicated strength or weakness in an opponent's hole cards.

These observation-impoverished individuals lack what pilots refer to as "situational awareness," a sense of where one is at all times; they don't have a solid mental picture of exactly what is going on around them. Ask them to go into a strange room filled with people, give them a chance to look around, and then ask them to close their eyes and report what they saw. You might wonder how they get around without a guide dog.

These are the persons who always seem to be blindsided by life's events.

>*"My wife just filed for divorce. I never had a clue she felt that way."*
>
>*"My son has been on drugs for five years; I had no inkling."*
>
>*"I was arguing with this guy and out of nowhere he sucker punched me. I never saw it coming."*
>
>*"The player across the table bluffed me out of a pot. How was I to know he had nothing?"*

These are the kinds of statements made by men and women who have never learned how to effectively observe the world around them. Such an inadequacy is not surprising, really. After all, as we grow from children to adults, we're never instructed on how to observe; there are no classes in elementary school, high school, or college that teach observation. If you're lucky, you teach yourself to observe the world; if you don't, you miss out on an incredible amount of useful information that could help you achieve your objectives in life.

But there's good news: observation is a skill that can be learned. Furthermore, because it is a skill, we can get better at it with the right kind of training and practice. And because observation is so critical to success at games like Texas Hold'em, this is where we must start our journey to poker's next level, that higher elevation where your enhanced ability to detect tells (and conceal your own) will increase your chances of winning at the tables.

The journey comes with a cost, however. It's going to take time and energy on your part to reach your destination. If you're not willing to make that commitment, then you're never going to reach your full winning potential as a poker player. In fact, all of the knowledge contained in this book will only be useful if you make a dedicated effort to utilize it at the tables. If you're going to play poker for money, I believe the cost is worth it.

Learning to Observe Effectively

Your success in reading people in a poker game is governed by your ability to effectively observe their behavior. Here are some steps you can take to become a more powerful observer.

1. **Make observation a way of life.** Effective observation is not a passive act. It is a conscious, deliberate behavior; something that takes effort, energy, and concentration to achieve and *constant practice* to maintain. The best way to become an effective observer, then, is to *conscientiously* observe your world at all times. Please don't delude yourself into thinking you can turn off your observation except when you're at the poker table. It doesn't work that way. You need to begin observing the minute you awake in the morning and begin interacting with the world around you. You've got to keep observing right up to the time you go to sleep at night. *Conscientious observation has to become a habit.* Once you train yourself to become a full-time observer in your everyday life, you'll be a more effective observer when you get to the poker table. Your observation will be more natural, more practiced, and you won't be overwhelmed by the sheer amount of information you'll need to process. It's amazing how much more you will notice once you've developed your observational skills through constant practice.

2. **Don't get out of the observational habit.** Observation—whether it be reading nonverbal tells at the table or watching what's going on around you as you walk down the street—is a perishable skill. If you stop using it, it will weaken, deteriorate, atrophy. Observing is a lot like speaking a second language or playing a sport: if you don't keep working at it, you're going to get rusty and your competency will decline.

3. **Sharpen your skills (or maintain a high skill level) by playing observation games.** Observational skills

improve and/or remain at high levels with practice, and one of the best ways to practice is the "recall game." This game can be played at any time, in any location, and as often as you wish. It involves observing something that occurs in your everyday behavior—say, walking into a room—and then closing your eyes and trying to remember, in as much detail as possible, whatever you saw. At first you'll find it difficult to recall much of anything. But as you continue to engage in this exercise, you'll be amazed at how much better you'll become at reconstructing an accurate mental picture of the physical environment you encountered. Not only will you remember more major objects in the environment, you'll also begin to recall smaller details as well.

I have played these games so frequently they have become an integrated, automatic part of my everyday observation. I have developed my "observation muscle" to a point where I can pay a visit to a friend at his or her home and, by the time I enter their front door, have an accurate mental picture of the immediate neighborhood: the type of vehicles parked on the street, a man mowing his lawn three doors away, a home where two newspapers lie in the driveway, a metal stake protruding from the middle of a worn section of lawn next door, and a lot across the street with one particularly green patch of grass along the side of the house.

I readily admit I have always been fascinated by what's going on around me, and, of course, I make my living studying the behavior of others, so my infatuation with playing observation games will probably exceed yours. Nevertheless, I think they are a great way to develop your visual powers, and also help you measure your progress toward observational excellence.

A second game, particularly useful for poker players, is the "what does this observation suggest" challenge. Once again, you are trying to observe and remember your surroundings but now, in addition, your challenge is to discover what "intel" (knowledge) you can gain from what you have seen around you.

Using the neighborhood visit I just described, what might I conclude from what I saw? (1) The man mowing the lawn probably lived in the house, as no commercial lawn maintenance vehicles were parked on the street; (2) the newspapers in the driveway suggested nobody had been home for the last day or two; (3) the metal stake in the middle of the worn section of lawn was probably a place where the neighbor kept his dog; and (4) the greener patch of grass across the street indicated the owner probably had a side-yard septic system.

In this game, it's fun to see if your hypotheses are correct, but even when they're not you're still sharpening your observational skills by learning to pay more careful attention to your surroundings and, at the same time, working to extract more information from what you see. Both these habits will serve you well at the poker table as you learn to observe your opponents more effectively and decipher what their behaviors really mean.

4. **Expand your observational range.** Some people have narrow-angle observation—they see what's directly in front of them, and that's pretty much the range of their worldview. Others have more wide-angle vision

and are able to expand the area that they observe. Obviously, the wider your observational field, the better. Wide-angle observation increases your chances of seeing things you might otherwise miss, gaining information you might otherwise lose.

Here's an experiment for you to perform. Stretch your arms straight out from your body, shoulder high, and turn your hands in. Now wiggle your fingers. If you can see them moving, this is your field of vision. If you can't see your fingers, then move your arms inward until you can. Once you spot your fingers, you'll know that's the potential visual field you can observe.

Many people don't take advantage of their full field of vision when it comes to observing. They limit their observation to what is directly in front of them— at the center of their viewing field, rather than expanding their range of sight to encompass their full viewing area. Learn to stretch your field of vision; life is more than what is directly in front of you! With practice, you will be able to look straight ahead and develop much wider sight lines. You'll be amazed by how much more you can see. This will be particularly valuable when you are at the poker table and want to observe more of your opponents without having to constantly turn your head and/or shift in your seat.

Effective Observation at the Poker Table

The major purpose of observation at the poker table is intelligence gathering—you want to learn as much as you can about each of your opponents at the table. Think of poker as a war and your opponents as your enemies. I want you to collect intelligence on every one of them because, should you have to face them in card-to-card combat, your intel might make the difference between victory and defeat.

Good intelligence gathering requires skilled observation, as you have to watch the actions of anywhere between one and nine other players, sometimes for hours at a time. In the following chapters, I will be telling you the specific behaviors you'll want to be looking for. This will make your job easier by narrowing the range of behaviors you need to observe, process, and remember. But it won't make your job simple! Far from it. The reality is, reading people at the poker table is flat-out hard work, and anybody who does it properly should be exhausted after a day at the tables.

Is it worth it? When you realize that 70 percent of poker success comes from reading the people and 30 percent from reading the cards, you decide. Just remember that most players already know how to play their cards (the mathematical and technical aspects of the game). Far fewer are competent in the people-reading skills we are examining. So, not only is reading people more important than reading the cards, only a small number of players can do it effectively. That gives you—if you can achieve proficiency in reading nonverbal communication—a double-edged advantage over most of your adversaries.

Players at my seminars often ask, "Joe, what is the best way to observe at the tables?" This is a good question, because inappropriate observation can sometimes do you more harm than good.

I recommend that you begin your observation the moment you get to the table, even if the game (or tournament) has yet to begin. When I take my seat, the first thing I do is look at the other players, trying to spot any information that might reveal their tells or style of play. Sometimes you might actually recognize a player. If you know who he or she is, you might also know something about how he or she plays. For instance, Gus Hansen is known as a superaggressive player. Well, if he were sitting at your table, that would be important information to know. I also notice how people are dressed. If I see people wearing poker apparel, I might conclude they are more knowledgeable and interested in the game than a guy who is wearing a shirt with the name of his insurance company emblazoned on the pocket. I might even ask the insurance guy, "Do you play often?" or "Is this your first tournament?" He might indicate he is a novice; again, important information to know. I try to see if I can spot any personality types: extravert, introvert, aggressive, conservative, timid. This might provide some insight into their style of play. Maybe I detect somebody who is the obsessive-compulsive type, chips meticulously stacked, card-guard positioned just so. This suggests that the person is probably regimented and might have predictable playing patterns.

I'm also looking for *baseline behaviors:* how people sit, where they place their hands, the position of their feet, their posture, their facial expression, even their normal chewing rate if they have gum in their mouth—anything that might help me read them more effectively when play starts. Establishing a player's baseline behavior is critical because it allows you to determine when he or she deviates from it, which can be very important. For example, if you note where your opponents usually place their hands on the table, then you'll be in excellent position to gain valuable information if, during critical phases of play, their hands move forward or retreat from where they are normally positioned.

Once the cards are dealt, I'm looking for specific behaviors that represent meaningful tells. These behaviors are called *generic tells* because they are exhibited by most players and usually for the same reasons. For instance, when a player is overprotective of her cards, and/or lofts her chips into the pot, she is probably sitting on a strong hand. As mentioned earlier, these generic tells will be described in the chapters to follow. I'm also looking for *idiosyncratic tells*, which are unique to a specific individual and might help me determine the strength of his hand or what he intends to do. For example, one well-known player uses his left hand to retrieve his chips if he intends to call a bet and his right hand if he plans to raise.

I'm continually collecting data and looking for *behavioral patterns*. If you see a person look at his cards, bite his lip, and then fold when it's his turn to act, you want to see if it's a random act or a reliable tell. If he does it again and again under the same circumstances, you can assume that this is valuable information you can use against him, remembering that *the best predictor of future behavior is past behavior.*

I'm also interested in watching my opponents for *multiple tells,* nonverbal behaviors that occur in clusters or in succession. This is because your accuracy in reading people will be enhanced when you have more than one tell to go on. It's like a jigsaw puzzle. The more pieces of the puzzle you possess, the better your chances of putting it all together and solving it correctly. If I see a player display a stress behavior followed by a pacifying behavior, I can be more confident she has a poor hand. The two behaviors together allow for a more accurate read on the cards she's holding. Similarly, if I see a player lean away from the table, it will mean one thing, but if that behavior is combined with that person placing his hands behind his head, it will mean something dramatically different. Again, the accuracy of your judgment will improve when you look for multiple tells *(tell clusters)*.

I'm always looking for *micro-gestures* during significant moments in the game (e.g., right after a person sees his or her cards). In these circumstances, the more reflexive and short-lived the behavior is, the more truthful it tends to be. If immediately after seeing a flop, a player quickly touches her fingers together (high-confidence gesture) and then shifts to hand-wringing behavior (low-confidence gesture), I'll go with the initial response and assume the person has a strong hand.

It's also important to look for *changes* in a person's behavior. Most poker players see someone shifting in her chair after a community card is dealt and they think, "Well, she's just uncomfortable." They miss the real possibility that when the player went from slouching to sitting erect, she was exhibiting engagement (going to get involved) behavior that suggests she suddenly feels a lot better about the cards she is holding.

Spotting *collaborative tells* in an opponent can also increase your confidence in the assessment you make. If you see an opponent put a large bet in the pot and then note that his legs are wrapped around his chair, he's holding his breath, he's remaining very still, and his hands are in a pious position, one can suspect that he's bluffing. He's literally scared stiff that he's going to be called.

Learning to detect *false* or *misleading tells* is also critical. The ability to make such discriminations takes practice and experience. I can help the process along by teaching you the subtle differences in a player's actions that reveal if a behavior is honest or dishonest, increasing your chances of getting an accurate read on your opponent.

The *intensity* of a tell is another significant component of accurately reading people that can be detected only through conscientious observation. As we will see in chapter 10, a half smile conveys information that is dramatically different from a full smile.

Observing tells in *context* will assist in deciphering their meaning. If I see a player's hands start to shake immediately after she sees her hole cards or the flop, I'll assume she is strong, because shaking is normally a sign of excitement associated with good cards. However, if the hand shaking doesn't occur in reaction to the cards dealt but, rather, after she pushes all her chips in, then I'll be more likely to assume she is bluffing. The context in which the shaking occurs makes a difference in how you interpret the behavior.

Finally, you need to observe *yourself*. This is the best way to make sure you are *concealing and not revealing* tells that would allow your opponents to get a read on you. If concealing your own tells is the only thing you learn from this book, you will already be light-years ahead of the vast majority of opponents you will face at the tables.

One thing you *don't* want to do when observing opponents is make your intentions obvious. What I see at the poker table is a lot of people staring at each other. Such intrusive observation is not advisable. If you're looking straight at a person and think you'll get an honest display out of them, well, that's just not going to happen. Your ideal goal at the table is to observe others without them *knowing* it. You want to be unobtrusive and subtle in your observation. Some of the older players like Doyle Brunson and John Bonetti have learned how to do this. It takes patience and practice, but you can do it, too. As you develop your observational skills, you will be able to gather information more quickly and less obtrusively, just as an experienced airline captain can quickly scan his cockpit instruments, whereas an inexperienced first officer needs more time to complete the same task, and his extended focus makes his behavior obvious.

If possible, you want to observe people as they look at their hole cards and, depending how far the hand is played, their reactions to any other cards dealt. Also, noting their responses to other significant behaviors at the table (calls, raises, reraises) can also prove helpful. You'll also want to be aware of their reactions to you: your play *and* your verbal comments.

As a hand plays out, a person's perception of his or her strength may change and be reflected in different nonverbal behavior(s). By noting a player's behavior from the start of the hand, you are in a position to glean significant information about what he is holding and intends to do by remembering the sequence of behaviors he displays as additional cards are dealt.

One of the best times to observe other players is when you are already out of the hand. *In fact, a good rule of thumb is to observe each hand at your table regardless of whether you are in or out of the action.* Sometimes it's easier to spot significant tells when you're not in the action because you can devote your full attention to everyone else at the table without the distraction of playing your own hand or worrying about when people will be looking at you (they won't be!). Some players get upset because they are dealt a hand they have to fold. I say, don't waste the opportunity the fold provides! Take advantage of this pressure-free time to get a read on your opponents. If you're fortunate enough to have folded when there are several people in the pot, this is a particularly advantageous time to gain significant information about your opposition. When you have multiple players in action, there's a lot more behavior out there for you to observe and, hopefully, use to your advantage in later play.

The same line of reasoning applies to tournament poker. I hear players complaining how they lasted through two days of the tournament and still didn't place in the money. I tell them, "That's looking at the glass half empty; why not look at it as half full? You were in action for all those hours and got a chance to collect information on numerous players that might prove very useful at some future point in time." In other words, view your tournament hours as "vacuum cleaner time"—a chance to absorb as much intel as you can for use in upcoming tournaments. Also keep in mind that those two days of tournament play provided you with a tremendous opportunity to hone your people-reading skills.

Decipher and Evaluate: Poker's Tells Revealed and Assessed

Once you have learned to observe behavior, the next crucial step is to decipher and evaluate it, determining which behaviors reveal significant tells and which ones can be ignored. The problem is that it could take you a lifetime of observation to make such a determination. Furthermore, it would be a colossal waste of time, since I've already done it for you! Through my 25 years of FBI experience and decades of studying nonverbal behavior, I've identified the specific behaviors that will provide the most worthwhile poker tells and analyzed their value at the tables. It is these specific behaviors I want you to watch for in your opponents.

This should make your observation at the tables more focused and manageable. My job is to describe these behaviors in enough detail so that you can readily identify them during play. This I will do in the following chapters. Your job is to conscientiously observe your opponents so you can spot these behaviors when they occur. Once you have trained yourself to recognize these nonverbal behaviors and can decipher and evaluate them based on the material in this book, you will be a force to be reckoned with whenever and wherever cards are dealt.

You are about to learn tells that have never been revealed in any other poker book. Some will surprise you. For example: if you had to choose the most "honest" part of the body—the part that would be most likely to reveal a person's *true* intentions— which part would you select? Take a guess. Once I reveal the answer, you'll know a prime place to look when attempting to put your opponent on a hand.

Respond and Enter in Database

Once you have conscientiously observed your opponents and deciphered/evaluated their actions, you are now ready to respond—take appropriate action at the table—based on what you have seen. Once this action is taken, you'll want to see if your decision was right or wrong: that is, whether your read on the other player(s) was accurate. This will provide you with continuing feedback on how you're performing and whether you need to make any adjustments to improve your people-reading capabilities. It will also give you information on the play of your opponents, information that could prove invaluable should you end up playing them again, either during the same session or at some future date.

One great way to increase your wins and your bankroll is to keep a database on your opponents. Most people don't have photographic memories; thus, if you spot some significant generic or idiosyncratic tells in other players, it is imperative you write them down so you won't forget what you've learned.

I recommend that you actually keep a log with the names of other players and relevant intelligence you've gathered on each of them. In the FBI, we evaluate every operation with a "post-action debrief." I suggest you do the same at the end of each playing session. Don't depend on your memory to recall what player did this or that—write it down. Obviously, the more often you play a specific opponent, the more detailed *and* valuable your database can become. One of the Camp Hellmuth participants who played against the same opponents every week cracked a game wide open by detecting their tells in just a few sessions.

In today's world of televised poker tournaments, a person can gather valuable information on various players for free. You don't have to risk your money against them; you simply have to turn on the tube and watch the action. I take delight in trying to spot a player's tells during these matches. It provides a challenge and a good opportunity to practice people-reading skills. It is amazing how much valuable information is out there for the taking and how many tournament professionals (final-table contestants!) exhibit tells that can be readily exploited by an alert opponent. Why not give it a try? Sit down with this book as a guide and attempt to detect the tells of any player at the table. With the added advantage of being able to see the players' hole cards, you can determine with certainty how they play various hands, which makes the identification of tells so much easier.

Don't underestimate the practice value you'll get from observing other players and trying to read them through their nonverbal behaviors. I think you'll be pleasantly surprised at how much easier watching and decoding behavior becomes as you spend more time doing it. Oh, and one last thing: if you spot something worthwhile about a specific player on TV, don't forget to enter it in your database. Who knows? That information might serve you well should you find yourself contesting a million-dollar pot against him or her at some future final table.

A Final Recommendation Before You Hit the Tables

If you want to become a serious threat at the poker table, you'll need to read people effectively. This involves learning how to (1) effectively and unobtrusively observe their behavior; (2) decode, in context, their actions, and incorporate that knowledge in your playing strategy; and (3) catalog their tells so you can utilize that information when playing them in the future.

It takes time to learn these skills; therefore, I would encourage you (particularly if you are a beginner) to enter the poker world in three stages.

1. Play for free at the online poker Web sites until you are comfortable with the rules and flow of the game. During this time, learn the math and the technical side of the game (learn to "read the cards").

2. Play small-stakes poker with friends or in low-limit games in brick-and-mortar casinos until you are comfortable in live (as opposed to computer) games. During this time, learn to observe the players, decode their tells, and keep a record of what you've discovered (learn to "read the players").

3. Once you feel comfortable playing poker in live games and have achieved a level of competency reading the cards *and* the players, then, and only then, should you consider playing for higher stakes at the tables.

Here is something to keep in mind. It's very difficult to spot tells when most of your attention is focused on getting to know the game. It's a lot like learning to drive. Do you remember the first time you gave it a go? If you were like me, you were so concerned with operating the vehicle that it was difficult to track what you were doing inside the car and concentrate on the road at the same time. It was only when you felt comfortable behind the wheel that you were able to expand your focus to encompass the total driving environment. That's the way it is with poker. Once you master the mechanics of the game and feel comfortable playing at the tables, then, and only then, can you free up the mental energy necessary to effectively read the cards *and* the people. As you approach and/or reach this comfort zone, you might want to learn more about tells: not only which ones are out there, but *what causes players to exhibit them in the first place*. Actually, learning what causes tells can help us deal with them more effectively, so we'll devote the next chapter to a discussion of that topic and move forward from there.

Phil's Thoughts on the Importance of Effective Observation for Winning at the Poker Table

Effective observation separates the winners from the losers at the poker table. It's that simple. It also separates the great players from the greatest players. When you have developed your powers of observation so you *know* that a player is weak or strong, it's almost like stealing. Your opponent might as well play with his cards face up.

In the foreword to this book, I mentioned how I liked to try to guess an opponent's hole cards. Observation plays an important part in this process. By the time someone has acted on his hand three or four times, a lot of information has been made available. How did he bet it before the flop? How much did he bet, and what did he seem to want his opponent to do in this hand? Did he look weak or strong? Exactly how weak or strong did he appear? What did he have the last time he acted this way? How did the flop alter his demeanor? Was he doing any acting that I see right through? And of course the cards on the board figure heavily in my assessments.

When you play, be sure to pay attention to the others at your table in order to gain insight into their play. Did they check-raise when they hit a big hand, or do they bet it? Try to sharpen up your reads on the opponents at your table—the kinds of reads we'll be presenting in this book. These reads will allow you either to make good moves on your opponents later, or to make good lay downs against them.

The more you practice your observational skills, the more proficient an observer you will become . . . even to the point of catching critical tells and/or information that others simply fail to see. Consider, for example, an incident that took place during the World Series of Poker (WSOP) in 2000. With 18 players left in the "Big One" (the $10,000 World Championship event), Hassan Habib, with over $600,000 in chips, raised the pot to about $25,000 to go with Ac–9c. Taso Lazarou called his last $25,000 or so with A–6 off suit. The hands were turned face up and everyone in the room (at least 200 people, including several tournament officials and the nine players at the table) saw or heard that the board came down 5-8-K-5-J. It was announced that Taso was eliminated, to finish eighteenth, at which point Taso got up from the table, the cards were turned facedown, and Hassan was awarded the pot.

After about 20 seconds (20 seconds is a long time in this case, especially since Hassan already had the chips in his stack), I informed Taso that it was actually a split pot. Taso went back to the table and announced that he thought it was a split pot and the pot was reconstructed and split accordingly.

Obviously if I hadn't said anything, the tournament would have continued on, with Taso in his car headed home. After the fourth card was turned up (5-8-K-5), I said to myself, "It will be a split pot if a face card is turned up." A face card, a jack, was turned up, and I announced out loud (several times) that it was a split pot. But, at that point, no one heard me.

The point here is that even when I wasn't in a hand I was still in the "observation mode" watching the action and anticipating what might happen given the possible playing scenarios. It allowed me to see things that other players missed, and when your observational skills allow you to do this more frequently than your opponents, you are going to be a winner in the long run.

The example I just cited should give you confidence when it comes to developing superior observational skills. If literally hundreds of accomplished poker players couldn't observe the split pot when it occurred, it suggests that if you make a serious

commitment to becoming an effective observer, you can probably reach parity with—and even superiority over—most amateur and professional players in a reasonable amount of time.
But it's going to take three things: practice, practice, and more
practice!

I firmly believe that the true champions of poker are blessed
with an observational talent that they hone through years of
practice and experience. Fortunately, very few of these "super"
observers exist (otherwise they'd dominate the poker world),
but to give you a feeling for what they can do, consider the story
of Stuey Unger. In the 1980s, Stuey was considered the best in
the world at gin (in fact, he was the best for two decades), the
best no-limit Hold'em player ever (by then he had won two
World Championships, with one more to come), and one of the
best backgammon players in the world as well.

During the WSOP in 1992, Stuey was playing in a five-
handed $600–$1,200 game on table 59, while Bobby Baldwin
and "Chip" Reese were playing gin at table 60. All of a sudden,
Chip turned to Stuey at the other table and said, "How did you
like the way I played that hand?" Stuey, who again was busy
playing $600–$1,200 at the adjoining table, said, "I would
have knocked four draws ago with five [points]." Chip then
said, "Thanks," and rolled his eyes back in his head.

Of course, Chip knew that Stuey was right, because Stuey
was considered all but unbeatable in gin. In fact, he was so good
at gin that for many years he couldn't even get a game from
anyone, anywhere. But Chip didn't roll his eyes back in his head
because Stuey was right. Rather, he rolled his eyes back because
he couldn't believe that Stuey was watching his every move
while simultaneously playing high-stakes poker at a completely
different table! Now, *that's* observation!

Chapter 2

The Physiological Foundation of Tells:
It's NOT a No-Brainer!

Take a moment, if you will, and bite your lip. Really, take a moment and do it. Now, touch your nose. Finally, stroke the back of your neck. These are things we do all the time. Sit at a poker table and you'll see players engaging in these behaviors on a regular basis.

Ever wonder *why* they do it? Ever wonder why *you* do it? The answer can be found hidden away in a vault—the *cranial vault*—where the human brain resides. Once we learn the answer, we'll also discover what causes tells and how to interpret them. So, let's take a closer look inside that vault and examine the most amazing three pounds of matter found in the human body.

A Brain That is Honest, a Brain That Can Lie

Most people think of themselves as having one brain. In reality, there are three distinct structures or brains inside our skulls, each performing specialized functions that, when taken together, form the "command-and-control" center that regulates everything our body does. Back in 1952, a pioneering scientist named Paul MacLean labeled these three distinct structures the "Triune Brain" and spoke of our "Reptilian [stem] Brain," "Mammalian [limbic] Brain" and "Human [neocortex] Brain" (see figure 1).

All behavior is controlled by the brain. *This is the cornerstone of understanding all nonverbal behavior.* There is nothing you do, be it a twitch or a scratch, that is not governed by the brain.

Fortunately, this is not a biology text, so I can spare you a detailed description of what the three brains do. In fact, I'm going to ignore what one brain (the Reptilian Brain) does altogether, give passing recognition to another (the Human Brain), and concentrate on the so-called emotional, Mammalian Brain, which plays the key role in the nonverbal behavior that underlies our tells.

When it comes to playing poker there are two brains that affect our play. We have the very ancient mammalian brain,

Human Brain

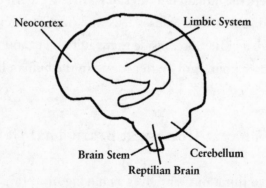

Neocortex   Limbic System

Brain Stem   Cerebellum
Reptilian Brain

Fig.1. The human brain and its major components.

sometimes called our limbic, emotional, or reactive brain. This primitive part of our brain, which we share with all mammals, has served to keep us alive as a species for millions of years. Its major function is to react to things that are heard, seen, sensed, or felt. It does so instantaneously, in real time, without thought; and, for that reason, it gives off an *honest* response to incoming information from the environment.

We also possess the *neocortex,* a relatively recent addition to the cranial vault. Also known as the thinking, intellectual, new, or human brain, it is responsible for higher-order cognition and memory. This is the brain that got us to the moon, with its ability to remember, compute, analyze, dissect, and intuit at a level unique to the human species. It is also the brain that helps poker players "read the cards": calculate pot odds, assess probabilities, determine our outs, and understand the rules of the game. Because it is capable of complex thought, this brain—unlike its limbic counterpart—is not necessarily honest; in fact, it is the least reliable of the three major brain components because this is the brain that can *lie.* While the limbic system may compel a person to squint (subconsciously) as an unsavory person walks by or an unfavorable card hits the table on fourth street, the cortex is quite capable of lying about true sentiments. The cortex, which governs Brocca's area (our speaking region), may cause us to say, "Hello, so very nice to see you," to the unsavory individual, even when it is an utter falsehood. Or worse, from a poker player's standpoint, it can lead a person to claim, "I've got the nuts," to an inquiring opponent when, in fact, the speaker is holding a busted flush.

Because the neocortex (the Thinking Brain) is capable of dishonesty, it is not a good source of reliable, accurate tells.

Furthermore, because it functions primarily as the center of intellectual activity—reading the cards—it's not relevant to the theme of this book. (There are already excellent books published for people who want to develop their card-reading ability.) As I pointed out earlier, according to poker experts, only 30 percent of tournament play is reading the cards, whereas 70 percent is reading people. Because the limbic system is where the action is when it comes to revealing honest tells that help us read people, this is where we want to focus our attention to gain that winning edge at the poker tables.

In Search of Limbic Reality

The beauty and downright elegance of the limbic system is that it reacts to the outside world immediately without having to conduct a lot of thinking and evaluation. For example, once the limbic system "sees" a dangerous river card that pairs the board and makes our flush vulnerable to a full house, it causes us to emit certain behaviors common to all human beings suddenly placed in perilous circumstances. Because the limbic system was designed *not to reason but to react,* these responses tend to be honest and revealing of a person's true feelings.

Conversely, the limbic system also works efficiently to register positive emotions. A discovery that your hole cards are pocket rockets (aces) will cause the limbic brain to "leak" behaviors that are consistent with an individual who has just seen something very favorable.

For those poker players who want to read their opponents effectively, the limbic brain is the Holy Grail of tells. Why? Because it is the brain that most honestly reveals the truth about the cards a person is holding. It does so through nonverbal behaviors that can be observed and decoded as they manifest physically in our feet, torso, arms, hands, and faces. And, unlike words, they are genuine. Furthermore, these responses are hardwired into our nervous system, making them difficult to disguise or eliminate—like trying to suppress a startle response when suddenly confronted with a loud noise.

One of the classic ways the limbic brain has assured the survival of our species—and produced a reliable number of poker tells—is by regulating our behavior when facing danger, whether it be a prehistoric man facing a Stone Age lion or a modern-day player facing a card-savvy shark with the stone-cold nuts.

The Three *F*s You Need to Know to Play Poker

You have probably heard or read the term "fight-or-flight response," which refers to the way we respond when faced with a threatening or dangerous situation. Unfortunately, this term is only two-thirds accurate and half-assed backward! In reality, the way living organisms—humans included—react to danger is in the following order: *freeze, flight, fight.*

The Freeze Response

A million years ago, as early hominids traversed the African savanna, they were faced with predators that could outrun and overpower them. For early man to succeed, the limbic brain, which had evolved from our reptilian forbearers, developed strategies to compensate for this predator power advantage. That strategy, or first response of the limbic system, was to *freeze* in the presence of a predator or a threat. Movement attracts attention, so by holding still immediately upon perceiving a threat, the limbic brain learned to react in the most effective fashion possible to ensure survival. Most animals—certainly most predators—react to, and are attracted by, movement. This ability to freeze in the face of danger makes sense.

The freeze response has been passed from primitive man to modern man and remains with us today as our first line of defense against a perceived threat or danger. You can see it in the showrooms of Vegas where big cats are part of the act. As the tiger or lion walks onto the stage, you can be sure that the people in the first row will not be making any unnecessary gestures—they will be frozen in their chairs.

You can see it at the poker table, too, particularly when a person is bluffing. Bluffers know they have a weak hand, and if they've got a sizable portion of their chips invested in the pot, this is threatening to them. Further, they don't want a call from their opponents (who, in this case, can be seen as predators who might attack their chips). So, what do they do? They freeze. They react just like our ancestors did a million years earlier. They freeze because they feel threatened and don't want to be noticed. They don't want to do anything that will call attention to them and make an opponent (predator) more likely to call their bet.

At the table, always assume that whenever anyone suddenly stops moving, freezes, or otherwise overcontrols (restrains) himself, he's bluffing. At the FBI, when someone behaves that way, we call it a clue. There's a threat out there, they've moved their chips into the pot, and now they're sitting ramrod straight like they're in a pilot's ejector seat, perfectly still, because they don't want to be noticed.

T. J. Cloutier commented at the first Camp Hellmuth poker seminar that he often detects bluffers because they hold their breath. This is a freeze response. Animals in the wild do it to reduce the chances they'll be observed. I also see it on polygraph exams: people that are going to lie stop breathing, and it shows up on the machine.

There is a tendency for bluffers to hold very still—to move less, to try to restrict any behavior that would heighten awareness of their physical presence at the table. Many players will demonstrate this bluff-bet-freeze behavior their entire poker lives and never be aware they are doing it. This is because it's the "natural" way to act, congruent with survival behaviors that have been hardwired into our stimulus-response patterns over hundreds of thousands of years.

This freeze behavior is so ingrained in our reaction to threat that some players can't stop doing it, even when told they're giving away bluffs by freezing. It is like habitual smokers who aren't even aware they have a cigarette in their hand unless someone continually points it out or they force themselves to constantly monitor their behavior.

I'm not saying that overcoming a freeze response during a bluff is impossible, just difficult. In fact, some people who read this book—and a few savvy players who have detected the response on their own—will attempt to eliminate it. Because we possess a neocortex, we can override limbic system responses if we *think* about it, but, with the exception of professional actors, not many people can actually do it convincingly. Oftentimes these cover-ups are painfully transparent . . . and with practice, you will usually be able to tell the difference between "true" and "false" tells with a high degree of success.

Consider the behavior of players who are trying to conceal

their freeze responses at the table. Their immediate response to their bluff is the honest one, a freeze-type behavior. They will then think to themselves, "I better start acting like everything is OK." What follows is a kind of excessive bantering and talking that acts as a cover for what is really going on. When this happens, I ask myself, "How did the player respond *immediately* after he/she first bluffed?" If it was a freeze response followed by a show of activity, I will trust the initial response, as it was likely the truest reflection of reality (it happened before the player had a chance to "think" about it).

Players who are trying to conceal a freeze response will often exhibit telltale signs that reveal their attempted deception. If the player makes a bet and then becomes more talkative and/or animated than normal, I become more convinced he or she is bluffing. This is particularly true if the player is usually very quiet and/or undemonstrative during play. If the talk seems forced or the movements exaggerated, I also become suspicious.

Because the freeze response is so deep-seated in our response to threats, players are often unable to monitor and change all the various behaviors associated with the freeze. Some remain, usually unnoticed by the player but detectable by the competent observer. For example, a player may feign an "unfrozen" response by moving his head, arms, and torso . . . but under the table he has his feet locked securely around the legs of his chair (a freeze response). When I observe these kinds of conflicting behaviors, I have a tendency to go with the ones that seem most honest (ones that are in keeping with the expected limbic response and/or are more consistent with the player's normal table demeanor). Those are usually the true tells.

The Flight Response

One purpose of the freeze response, as noted, was to avoid detection by dangerous predators. A second purpose was to give the threatened individual the opportunity to assess the situation and determine the best course of action to take. If the freeze response was not adequate to eliminate the danger, the second response of choice was to get away through *the flight response*. In the presence of a predator or at a poker table—whenever we face something we don't like—our reaction is the same: we want to get away from it. Thus, at the poker table—and in life—we equate flight with *distance*.

Whereas it is practical and judicious to run from a hungry lion if you find yourself being stalked on the Serengeti, a headlong dash from the poker table when facing some hungry card shark is both impractical (don't try running through a casino!) and a serious breach of etiquette. Not to worry! The limbic brain has developed other unique techniques to deal with threats that don't involve headlong flight, techniques involving more subtle behaviors that either block or distance a person from a perceived danger.

If you think back on the social interactions you've had in your life, you will recognize that you lean toward those you like and away from those you don't. The same holds true at the poker table: you'll draw nearer to the table (or your cards or chips) when you have a great hand and draw back when your hole cards are bad or, worse, when a good hand turns ugly (see figures 2 and 3). These are modern manifestations of the ancient flight response, more subtle but still revealing to the observant eye. Why do we do it? Because for millions of years we have

Fig.2. Leaning in; most likely a good hand.

Fig.3. Leaning away; a marginal or poor hand.

withdrawn from anything we don't like; we walk (or run) out of the room, walk out of their lives, or lean away. When you see bad cards in your hand it's no different: the brain is saying, "Why should I allow my arms to linger here at the table when I have a crap hand? Let's do what we've always done to protect you—withdraw."

One thing you'll want to do when you enter a poker game is note where your opponents normally place their hands and/or arms on the table (see figure 4). Once this is determined, you can use deviations in hand/arm movements from their standard location as a yardstick to assess the strength of your opponent(s) cards. (Even if you don't know the normal hand/arm position of a player, you should be aware whenever she shifts her hand or arm position toward or away from the table during the play of a hand. This might help you determine the strength of her cards.)

Sometimes you'll witness a player exhibiting hand/arm

Fig.4. Normal hand location at the table.

withdrawal *and* approach during the play of a single hand. For instance, you might observe that while a player checks his hole cards, his arms will move forward on the table. Then he'll see the flop and his arms will pull back, like a turtle retreating into its shell. Or maybe his arms will remain stationary on the flop and then advance further or withdraw on fourth and/or fifth street. Taken alone, or in combination with other tells, you can use this information to get a better read on what your opponent is holding. For example, note how the player's arms move forward from their "baseline" position (figure 5), after the player views his hole cards (figure 6), the flop (figure 7), and fourth street (figure 8). One can assume from this behavior that he is becoming increasingly pleased with his hand with each new card dealt.

Fig.5. This is the "baseline" position of the player's hands before any cards are dealt.

Fig.6. Note how the player's hands shift slightly forward after he views his hole cards, an indication that he likes what he sees.

Fig. 7. Hands move in closer as the flop improves the player's chances of winning.

Fig. 8. Hands continue their forward movement as a favorable turn card further strengthens the player's potential for winning the pot.

Have you ever watched a young child at the dinner table? The child, without benefit of a guidebook or directions, comes equipped to communicate nonverbally its likes and dislikes. For example, when the child's torso stiffens away from the dinner table and the feet turn toward the nearest exit, the message is clear: the child wants to get away from the table, to distance himself from the threat of food he finds distasteful.

It is no different at the poker table. Just as the child turned away from the food at the table, the player may shift away from an offending hand or a threatening flop. Blocking behaviors may also be manifested; the threatened player may close or rub her eyes, or place her hands in front of her face. She may lean away from the table and turn her feet away as well, sometimes in the direction of the nearest exit. These are not behaviors of deception but, rather, actions that signal a person feels threatened by events taking place around her. They are *distancing* nonverbal behaviors that tell you the player is unhappy with what is occurring at the table. Based on what is actually taking place, such flight responses could indicate a desire to get away from an abusive player, a destructive hand, or even the need to get to the bathroom. To determine the exact cause of the behavior, you need to watch when it occurs and the context in which it takes place. If the distancing behavior happens immediately after a player looks at her hole cards or a community card hits the table, one could reasonably conclude that the player does not like the cards she is seeing. It would suggest a weak hand or a hand that the player feels is vulnerable because of other cards on the table. It is unlikely that the player would defend such a hand, and would probably fold, particularly if facing an opponent's raise.

I recently watched a televised final table where the following behavior took place. One of the five remaining players looked at his hole cards and shifted his torso closer to the table. This is a tell of *high confidence* and *intention* that suggested two things: he liked what he saw, and he probably would get involved in the hand. Actually, he was one of three players who bet and saw the flop. Immediately upon seeing the community cards exposed, the player leaned away from the table—that is, he *distanced* himself from what he observed. The limbic brain, in essence, was telling him to "disengage . . . what is in front of you is no longer any good, it is dangerous." In evolutionary terms, a card, or cards, that can lose a player money is akin to a predator who can do him physical harm. It will elicit a flight response. Once you understand how the limbic brain works, it's very easy to pick up on the player's tell and decipher it, particularly when you consider how the behavior *changed* from the start of the hand through the flop and the context in which it occurred (immediately after the player saw the cards).

The limbic brain, once in the flight mode, causes us to function according to this basic strategy: we distance ourselves from anything that is disagreeable, unpleasant, dangerous; we draw nearer to anything that is agreeable, pleasant, rewarding. In the televised poker action just described, the player moved away from the table because the flop was not to his liking; it was distasteful and represented a threat to his financial well-being. The opposite kind of behavior occurs when a player sees something at the table she feels good about. Holding the ace and 10 of diamonds, she watches the flop come 4d, 8d, Qd, making her a nut flush. Her response is immediate: her torso shifts forward and her hands edge further onto the table. She might pay more attention to her hole cards, placing her hands around them caringly and protectively like a mother bird who shows increasing care for her eggs as they approach maturation. She is unaware that she's transmitting how excited she is about her hand. To her observant opponent, her behavior is a flashing neon sign blinking "Fold!" "Fold!" "Fold!"

The Fight Response

When a person confronts danger and can't avoid detection by freezing or escaping (flight), the only alternative left is to fight. At the poker table, the fight response often takes the form of *aggression*—players will argue, exchange insults, goad each other, engage in staredowns, and even invade an opponent's territory by "accidentally" sticking an elbow or a cup in his or her area of the table.

Why do players engage in this game of aggression/intimidation at the tables? Some do it because their chip count is getting low, or they're gambling more than they can afford to lose, or they've suffered a bad beat. Others do it to try to put you off your game. Remember when you were young and some kid would try to annoy you by making faces at school or on the playground? Not much has changed! The aggressive player still wants to annoy you, but this time he doesn't want your attention, he wants your money.

Sometimes a player will act aggressively toward an opponent because he wants to deter that player from entering a pot. Often this is done by glaring at the opponent when it's their turn to act (see figure 9). Depending on the circumstances, such staring could be a *managed tell* that would encourage the savvy player to do exactly the opposite of what the aggressor desires: it could serve as a sign to go ahead and bet, even raise. One needs to observe a player over many hands to determine if his hostile stare is, in fact, a way to keep opponents out of the pot

Fig. 9. Staring aggressively to intimidate—avoid it!

or just an attempt to intimidate opponents in general. As a general rule, the more frequently a person engages in staredown behavior, the more likely it represents a general playing style; the more selective the staring, the higher the chances it could be a significant tell worth considering as you ponder how to best play your hand.

In general, I advise poker pros and amateurs alike to refrain from aggressive play at the tables. Just as the *fight response* is the act of last resort in dealing with a threat—used only after the freeze and flight tactics have proven unworkable—so, too, should it be avoided in your game whenever possible. Reserve your mental energy for reading the cards and the people rather than posturing and puffing out your chest.

There is a reason for this recommendation. Aggressive play at the tables can lead to emotional turmoil in the affected players, making it difficult to concentrate and play one's best game. When we are emotionally aroused, our neural activity is diverted, and we are handicapped because of it. I have a theory about this: one of the reasons I believe women do so well in poker tournaments (ending up at final tables in greater proportion than their numbers would justify) is because they don't engage in as much aggressive behavior as their male counterparts. While men are depleting themselves in testosteronic warfare, snarling and staring and playing their mind games, the ladies are saving their energy to play poker games, keeping their cool and using their brainpower to win pots rather than intimidate opponents.

In the United States, by social convention, we are entitled to look at another person for only 1.18 seconds before our stare is interpreted as a challenge or an invitation. If you're trying to play your best game of poker and you run across an opponent who is trying to intimidate you through hostile staring or other forms of aggression, what should you do?

Ignore him. Usually, he will focus his energy elsewhere. If he doesn't, avoid eye contact with him whenever possible. Whatever you do, don't get into eye-to-eye combat; that's just playing into his game and destroying yours. If necessary, you can wear sunglasses at the table. This tends to discourage opponents from staring at you because (a) they can't tell where you are looking, and (b) they can't learn as much information (for example, if their staring behavior is successfully unsettling you).

While we're on the topic of visual aggression in poker, I'd like to warn the women that they, too, can be a target of male intimidation at the tables. Some men will attempt to disrupt a woman's game by staring at her breasts, assuming, correctly at times, that this will make the lady embarrassed and uncomfortable, disrupting her concentration and playing effectiveness in the process (see figure 10). As in the case of male-to-male aggressive staring, there's not much that can be done about this. Ignoring the offending players and their boorish behavior is probably your best defense. Once these players realize that their distasteful strategy is not working, they will usually focus their attention, and their eyes, elsewhere.

Some aggressive players will attempt to rattle you by physically moving themselves or objects (cups, drinks) into your area of the table. If they do this, ask them politely to move further away and remove any of their drinks and belongings from your playing territory (see figures 11–13). If they don't comply, you have every right to call over a floor manager, whether it be in a tournament or casino cash game, and lodge a complaint.

Fig.10. Intimidation of women
by looking at their breasts.

Fig.11. Intimidation through
territorial violations, in this
case with a cup.

Fig.12. Intimidating with your body—normal elbow posture.

Fig.13. Intimidating players using your elbows.

Don't let their harassing behavior get you ruffled; the moment it does, they've gained the upper hand and will probably beat yours as well.

Abusive verbal remarks—insults, taunts, and challenges—comprise another form of aggressive behavior used to fluster players and knock them off their game. Sometimes verbal behavior is not abusive but, rather, an approach used by savvy players to get a line on the strength of the cards you're holding. I have seen Phil Hellmuth use this tactic to good advantage numerous times. In one tournament, I saw Phil ask another player who had just raised him, "Whatcha got there?" The guy meekly looked down and bit his lip (a low-confidence behavior combined with a pacifying action, normally indicative of a bluff). Phil caught him; he was, indeed, bluffing. Phil's verbal challenge was enough to disarm his opponent. On another occasion, Phil asked his opponent the same question ("What have you got there?"), and this time the response he got was "I've got a good hand." Problem was, when the player replied, his voice cracked, a classic verbal tell of low confidence. That person's verbal behavior provided the tell Phil needed to determine that his opponent was bluffing.

Whether an opponent is trying to use abusive verbal remarks to compromise your playing effectiveness or asking questions to assess your hand strength, your response should be the same: *ignore the comments and remain silent.* Do not get embroiled in verbal sparring or revealing tells through your speech. To paraphrase the title of an old submarine movie, "Play silent, play deep." And, while we're on the topic of seagoing vessels, remember the old World War II adage "Loose lips sink ships." At the poker table, loose lips can sink chips! Of course, playing this noncommunicative style will not make you the most popular or friendly person at the table. Therefore, it's *not* a style I'd recommend when you're playing socially at the weekly small-stakes poker game back home. But when big money is at stake, when you're playing *serious* poker, you should be quieter than a church mouse at the school library.

One shouldn't feel an obligation to be sociable and talkative when playing high-stakes poker. It's more important to conceal tells than win a popularity contest when big money and skilled players come together at the table. Annie Duke is a great role model for this kind of play. Away from the game, she is talkative, gregarious, and funny, but when she sits down at the poker table she's all business. She's not there to socialize and converse; she's there to do her job in a no-nonsense fashion. That's one reason for her continuing success in the biggest poker games and tournaments in the world.

A Final Note on Our Limbic Legacy

In this chapter, we have learned that all behavior is governed by the brain. We have examined the "thinking brain," the neocortex, and the "emotional brain," the limbic system. Both brains perform important functions, but for our purposes, the limbic system is more critical because it is the most *honest* brain and is responsible for producing the most significant tells at the poker table.

In understanding how the limbic brain functions, we studied three critical survival functions and their associated behaviors, which you need to know and understand to play poker effectively.

Freeze = Overcontrol, restraint, stillness
Flight = Distancing, blocking behaviors, grimacing
Fight = Aggressive play, intimidation, disrespect

There is one aspect of our limbic legacy I failed to mention, until now. The *degree* or *intensity* of our limbic response is in large part determined by the perceived significance of the stimuli in our world. If we're hiking in a state park and come across a stray house cat, our limbic arousal will be minimal. The animal doesn't present a viable threat or danger. If, on the other hand, we chance upon a wild mountain lion, our primitive survival mechanisms will kick in and our limbic brain will cause us to freeze and then, if necessary, take flight or fight.

The same is true at the poker table. If you are playing in a nickel-dime-quarter home game, your limbic responses will be minuscule. The effect of losing $10 or $20 is just not substantial enough to engage our emotional brain. In big games, however, where considerable money is involved (particularly tournaments where millions of dollars are at stake), you're going to see significant limbic responses and the tells they produce. In a sense, then, the bigger the game, the greater the tells . . . and the greater the tells, the bigger your profits if you can read people effectively.

Is Detecting Tells All That Easy?

This is one of the most frequent questions I'm asked when running seminars on poker tells. The answer is yes and no. Once you've read this book, some tells will stand out—they literally scream for attention. This is why many of the Camp Hellmuth participants were able to go to the casino poker tables after an hour of instruction and make significant money. They could spot those easy tells and take advantage of them. On the other hand, there are many tells that are far more subtle and will take the kind of *conscientious observation* discussed in the previous chapter to detect and decipher. We will be presenting and examining these tells in later chapters of this book.

What If I Don't Want to Make the Effort Necessary to Read People Effectively?

The simple answer is that you won't do as well at the poker table. However, there is still something you can do to enhance your game. If you decide that becoming proficient in reading people requires too much work, then let me make this request: please don't stop reading just yet. Finish the next chapter. Once you've completed that material, you can close the book forever and get on with your life. But read that chapter first! If you learn nothing more than what is contained in those pages, it will significantly reduce your losses at the table because people won't be taking advantage of your nonverbal tells to beat you out of your money. And, best of all, what I'll be asking you to do is not very difficult to achieve.

Chapter 3

Learn to Conceal, Not to Reveal!

There are two ways that nonverbal behaviors (tells) can impact your financial well-being at the tables.

1. You can *make* money by using your opponents' tells to play more effectively against them.
2. You can *save* money when opponents can't use your tells to play more effectively against you.

This brings us to *Navarro's Axiom: To save your money, learn to conceal and not reveal.* Even if you are a poor reader of other people's tells and learn nothing more from this book than what is contained in this chapter, you can still preserve a lot of your chips if you learn to conceal the majority of your tells (the more, the better) from other players at the table. The less you reveal, the more sharks miss their meal!

To accomplish the objective of this chapter, I'm going to have to persuade some of you that concealing tells is important and convince you to take the steps necessary to achieve that concealment. This is because some of you subscribe to one or more of the following misconceptions.

1. *Concealing tells is not that important because most people don't look for them in the first place.*

   Because so much poker success comes from reading people, as opposed to knowing how to play the cards, you can be assured that there is plenty of scrutinizing for tells at the tables. There is also a growing awareness in the poker community concerning the critical role of tells in effective play. In speaking with players at all levels of experience and skills, there is near unanimity about the need for spotting tells at the tables—and the popularity of the topic at poker seminars and camps speaks to the willingness of players to learn about, and look for, tells in their opponents.

2. *Even if players did look for poker tells, discovering them wouldn't provide the kind of information that would help a person win more money at the tables.*

   Players who believe this statement are tasty morsels on the low end of the food chain. Forget about the card sharks, these individuals are easy prey for poker minnows: individuals who are just starting to play but are serious about winning. This is why Camp Hellmuth participants, after only 60 minutes of instruction on spotting tells, were able to win thousands at the Las Vegas poker tables in a matter of hours. People who make no effort to conceal their tells might just as well give their money away, because they're in for a major money hemorrhage at the poker table.

3. *Most players don't have tells, thus, there's no need to conceal them.*

This is very dangerous thinking, because players who don't think they have tells aren't going to work at eliminating them. The fact is, we all have tells. Everybody. Pro, amateur, beginner, veteran—it doesn't matter. Nobody is devoid of tells, although some players have more than others. With the appropriate effort, each of us can have fewer tells tomorrow then we do today.

All this being said, I hope you are willing to conceal any tells you might be revealing at the tables. I'll recommend a technique for doing it in a moment. What's important to remember is that even if you can't conceal *all* your tells, any reduction in their number—particularly the obvious tells—will save you money in the long run.

Adopting a Robotic Approach to Your Table Image

I'd like you to imagine a robotic arm at an auto assembly plant. Time after time, day after day, month after month, year after year, it continues to do the same thing the same way. Its performance is a masterful depiction of relentless repetition, a behavior that never changes, an action that recurs over and over and over again. An observer could get bored pretty quickly watching such a machine. It wouldn't take long before he had seen enough and shifted his attention elsewhere.

This is exactly what we want to shoot for at the poker table! I want to teach you a highly stylized, repetitive, information-concealing routine for presenting yourself and handling your cards at the table. If this can be accomplished, you will gain two tremendous advantages at the table.

1. You will minimize the number of tells you give away at the table.
2. Because your table behavior is repetitive and never varies, opponents will quickly become bored with observing you and will look elsewhere for more interesting players to observe.

What you need to do, then, is develop a robotic (automatic, repetitive) approach to handling your cards and wagers that is consistent and conceals your nonverbal behaviors. You want to become so repetitive that you fly under the radar of human interest. You want people to grow tired of looking at you because there's nothing to pick up, because nothing has changed, because they've seen it all before. Also, by adhering to a rigid, repetitive table behavior, you go a long way to eliminating tells that might occur if your table behavior was more flexible.

In the photographs on the following pages, I have provided you with a methodology for dealing with your cards and establishing a proper table posture. Study the pictures along with the description I'll be providing. Then practice playing this way at the tables. If you can maintain this behavioral approach in your play, you will be a difficult read and, in the final analysis, a person of little interest at the table . . . *exactly* what you want to be.

A Step-by-Step Guide to Establishing
Your Table Image

1. When you sit down at the table, take time to get ad-
    justed in your seat. You will want to assume a posture,
    sitting position, and distance from the table that is
    easy and comfortable to maintain for long periods of
    time. Your goal will be to maintain your sitting pos-
    ture and position with as little deviation as possible
    (see figure 14).

2. Arrange your chips in neat stacks so they can be easily
    seen and totaled by you, the dealer, or another player
    (by looking). Maintain a neat chip stack throughout play.

3. When you receive your hole cards, you will want to
    look at them the same way every time. I recommend you
    look at your cards with your head low. This gives away
    less information. Try to see the cards without actually
    picking them up, so as not to give away any possible
    hand movements. Once you observe your cards, don't
    look up; continue to look down. Try to retain the same
    facial expression regardless of the cards you observe.
    Also, try to look at your hole cards for the same amount
    of time each time a hand is dealt (see figure 15).

4. When you have finished looking at your hole cards,
    cup your hands together, one atop the other, and bring
    them up to your mouth level. Then sit up (see figures
    16–19) with your elbows slightly out and your hands
    over your mouth. Maintaining this position will make
    it difficult for an opponent to observe your eyes or de-
    tect any mouth or nose tells. At the same time, you're
    blocking most of the area of the neck that might reveal

Fig.14. Find and use a comfortable sitting position.

Fig.15. Initiate a routine or robotic process
for initially looking at cards.

Fig. 16. Routinely examine the cards, face low.

Fig. 17. Do not vary from the routine—keep your hands together in front of you.

information about what you have, and, by keeping your hands cupped in a specific position, you are reducing tells that involve them and their movements to other areas of your body and/or the table.

5. Strive to retain the same posture and distance from the table throughout the hand.

6. When you bet, know what you're going to do before you do it. Keep your verbal announcements short and consistent over the length of your play. Always move your chips into the pot in the same manner with a simple statement such as "call," "raise," "reraise," or "all-in." Once you have moved your chips to the pot, immediately return to your standard hands-cupped-over-mouth sitting position.

Fig.18. Fix your routine position, hands together
and blocking the mouth.

**Fig.19. Maintain your position as part of the routine;
eventually, others will ignore you.**

7. Do not make extraneous movements in any part of
    your body—your legs, torso, hands, arms, face—during
    play of the hand. If you need to shift in your seat,
    scratch your neck, yawn, lick your lips, or move about
    and stretch to get more comfortable, do so *between*
    hands or during hands you are not playing.

8. Try to maintain the same facial expression throughout
    play.

9. Remain as noncommunicative as possible at the table,
    both during and between hands. Do not engage in
    conversation or eye contact with other players unless
    absolutely necessary. Remember, your verbal and eye
    behavior can provide an opponent with valuable tells.

10. If a player asks you for a chip count, you can make an
    easy assessment because you have kept your stacks

neatly piled and segregated by denomination. Without touching the chips, if possible, make your count and then, without looking at the player, simply announce the total.

11.   Remember that your limbic brain is affecting your behavior just as it does the actions of your opponent. By retaining the same posture, table distance, and hand behavior, you reduce the likelihood of giving off a limbic response, but you don't eliminate it. Try to retain a normal breathing pattern, even when executing a bluff. Keep your feet flat on the floor. Try to keep your voice and your hands steady.

12.   Repeat the same behavior, hand after hand after hand. This is critical to minimizing your tells and maximizing the chances that other players will soon ignore you and turn their attention to other opponents with more interesting body language. Does this make for good television? No. If everyone acted robotically, most viewers would reach for the remote to change channels. But remember, your goal at the table is to win money, not an Oscar. If restricting your movements means you are preserving your assets, so be it. To paraphrase the old nursery rhyme, you be "one for the money" and let the others be "two for the show"; that way, you'll be "free to play steady" and not "forced to go."

Will I Have Difficulty Concealing My Tells?

People are different, so it should come as no surprise that some individuals have an easier time concealing their tells than others.

Some players give away more tells to begin with and will have a greater challenge in concealing them. Individuals also vary in how much effort they are willing to expend in concealing their nonverbals. Those who are committed to the task and work hard at it are more likely to see successful results in a shorter period of time. But the bottom line is this: concealing, not revealing is an attainable goal. Consider the case of Alice Thompson (not her real name). She was a participant in the first Hellmuth poker camp and was a virtual "tell transmitter"—she gave off tells like a nuclear isotope gives off radiation. Players were taking advantage of her at the tables, using her tells to call her down when she was bluffing and to fold against her strong hands. I pulled the woman aside and spent about 10 minutes pointing out her most obvious tells. I told her she squinted at her cards when she had a rag hand and tightened her jaw when the flop didn't go her way. Then I suggested ways (described in this chapter) she could conceal her tells. By the end of the next day, she had improved her play so dramatically that she made the final table of the special camp tournament! She had changed her demeanor completely and become a tough read. You might not achieve Alice's results as quickly as she did, but, with commitment, you can accomplish what she did.

Verifying the Accuracy of Your Table Image

OK, so you've come up with your best concealing profile at the table that cuts down on your nonverbal tells and encourages your opponents to look elsewhere for useful information. The question is, how can you assess the adequacy of your new table image? One way, of course, is in actual game conditions at the table, but that can be expensive and stressful . . . particularly if your image needs some fine-tuning. I recommend you treat the development of your new table image like an actor practicing to perform in a play. First, you need to rehearse your role before you appear live on stage. Then you need the feedback of someone you can trust when it's time for your dress rehearsal.

Here is how I'd proceed. In the first stage, I'd purchase, borrow, or rent a video recorder. These days, such equipment is not that expensive. Set it up on a tripod and play a game with some friends at your home. Keep the camera focused on yourself and let it run for a few hours while you're playing. Make sure you sit at the end of the table so that the camera can capture your entire body as you play. Then go back and take a look at what's been recorded and ask, "What do I see here?" Just as we are often shocked when we first hear our spoken voice on a recording, most individuals are amazed when they see themselves on camera for the first time and realize how certain parts of their body are giving off nonverbal tells that reveal their intentions and hand strength without their realizing it. Your reward for making this effort should be evident after a few hours of filming. You'll probably be able to spot most of your tells that other people can see and utilize to their advantage. Now you'll be in a position to eliminate these giveaway behaviors and present a more concealed image at the table.

In the second and final phase of this exercise, I'd pick a poker friend that you can trust, an individual who has read this book and is familiar with tells, and ask him to watch you play at your home game. Ask him to see if he can spot any tells in your behavior at the tables. If he can, you can make further modifications; if he can't, then you're probably ready for the curtain to go up on your real casino performance with your new poker-table persona. Just remember not to let the higher stakes change you back to your old tell-revealing self. When significant amounts of money are involved, it will always be more difficult to conceal your limbic-driven behaviors. Also, monitor yourself at regular intervals (or have your friend give you periodic "checkups") to make sure your old nonverbal habits have not made an untimely reappearance. That said, let the play begin!

What About the Use of Sunglasses to Conceal Behavior?

Sunglasses can be a very effective way of concealing, not revealing—thus, I would recommend them for players who feel they need them. Ever wonder why agents of the U.S. Secret Service wear sunglasses? There are actually two reasons: so people can't see where they're looking; they make the wearer seem more unfriendly and, therefore, they don't have to deal with as many people approaching them. I'd add a third possible reason: they are intimidating, making the wearer seem more in control and authority.

These aren't bad reasons for wearing sunglasses at the table, particularly if your goal is to conceal and not reveal. If an opponent can't see where you're looking, there's less of a chance for a visual confrontation and the possible outbreak of aggressive behavior at the table. Furthermore, if you seem more unfriendly, it will reduce the probability that other players will engage you in conversation, an outcome that is desirable for a player seeking to mask rather than divulge information. Finally, if you can sustain an image of intimidation at the table, it is less likely that other players will play mind games with you, leaving you to retain your cloak of anonymity.

There are other reasons to wear sunglasses, too. They can block a lot of visual tells, such as change in pupil size (more easily spotted in people with green and blue eyes), eye-orbit variation, and eyebrow arching. The advantage of blocking these tells should not be underestimated. At the poker seminar, Phil related an incident in which he spotted an opponent raising his eyebrows when he saw his cards—a *high-confidence* tell. Phil wisely folded his hand and saved a lot of money because his opponent had the nuts.

How About Throwing In a Hat for Good Measure?

Again, this depends on the person. There are some people who give away so much in their faces that it just blows me away. I suggested to one lady poker player that she get herself a visor because I was reading her facial tells three tables away. Every time she got a bad hand, she would furrow her brow and roll her eyes. Collectively, these are known as *dismissive tells*. And sure enough, each time she exhibited the behaviors, she threw her hand away. She might as well have raised her hand and said, "I'm going to fold!" If you're like that lady, then get a visor or hat and keep your head low . . . you're too easy to read.

All of these clothing accessories do bring up an interesting question, of course. Where do we draw the line? Should we all play like Phil Laak, "the Unabomber," with his hooded sweatshirt covering most of his face? What about a mask that would cover the entire area of the head? There was a guy wearing an Elmo outfit at the World Series of Poker. I'm sure it helped hide his tells. Is that appropriate? Maybe everyone should come

dressed in a burka, with just a slit in the outfit for the eyes (which could be covered by sunglasses). That could eliminate a large majority of tells and almost get you to the point where you might as well be playing online.

Does playing with tell-blocking accessories give some players an unfair advantage?

Yes.

Will anything be done about it? I don't know. Perhaps at some future date, all major tournaments will be played with a uniform set of rules regulating what a person can and cannot wear at the tables. This would be the fairest way to deal with the issue; it would put everyone on the same footing. Until that time comes—if ever—I suggest that each player judge for himself if accessories like sunglasses and hats can help him conceal and not reveal. If his assessment is affirmative, then I say put 'em on. Any legal edge at the table is worth exploiting, particularly in tournament poker, where revealing or concealing one tell can make a difference worth millions of dollars.

A Concealment Tack From the Man in Black

A solid poker player must always be careful not to give off tells; otherwise, he risks financial ruin from those observant enough to detect them. This requires that you consistently monitor your game to make sure you haven't picked up any tells along the way and that, when necessary, you use "props" to reduce the probability that tells will be spotted even when you give them away.

There are several steps I take to reduce the chances of giving off tells during play and/or making them more difficult to detect should I reveal them during the course of a hand. Wearing dark glasses helps conceal eye tells. My trademark "fists in front of my face" position protects me from revealing mouth tells. I also usually wear a dark black jacket that I zip all the way up so opponents can hardly see any of my neck or chin. I also work hard at checking in the same manner whether weak or strong. Finally, I usually wear a hat that is pulled low over my forehead to further conceal any facial tells that might reveal the strength of my hand.

Chapter 4

The Most Honest Part of Your Body

Back in chapter 1, I asked you to guess the most "honest" part of the body—the part that would be most likely to reveal a person's *true* intentions and, thus, be a prime place to look for tells when attempting to put your opponent on a hand.

The answer is . . . your feet!

That's right, your feet win the honesty award hands, uh, feet down.

"But," you protest, "even if that is true, what good is it? I can't see an opponent's feet under a poker table."

Well, actually you can under certain circumstances. And, besides, there are more effective ways to determine foot behavior than peeking under the table. I'll explain how this can be done in a few moments, but first I want to tell you *why* your feet are the most honest part of your body. In doing so, you'll get a better appreciation for why the feet are such good candidates for poker tells and why they behave the way they do.

An Evolutionary Footnote

For millions of years, our feet and legs have been our primary means of locomotion, and the principal means by which we have survived. Marvels of engineering, our feet provide a platform that allows us to feel, walk, turn, run, swivel, balance, kick, climb, play, grasp, and even write. And while not as efficient at certain tasks as our hands (we lack an opposable big toe), nevertheless, as Leonardo da Vinci once commented, our feet are so exquisitely designed as to be a testament to God's handiwork.

Our feet and legs accommodate whatever thought is in our heads. When we want to run, our feet adapt for the chore; when we want to jump, they don't let us down. When a boat rocks, they help us balance; when we feel threatened, our feet will immediately prepare to escape. As the writer and zoologist Desmond Morris once observed, our feet communicate exactly what we think and feel more accurately and more honestly than any other part of our bodies.

Why are the feet and legs such accurate reflectors of our sentiments? For millions of years, long before we spoke a common language, our legs and feet reacted to environmental threats (fires, snakes, lions) instantaneously, without the need for conscious thought. Our limbic brains made sure that our feet and legs reacted as needed by either freezing motion, running away, or by kicking at a potential threat. This survival feature, common to all hominids, has served us well. This finely tuned system is so sensitive that when we are presented with something dangerous or even disagreeable, our feet and legs still react the same way. They freeze first, attempt to distance second, and finally, if no other alternative is available, prepare to fight and kick.

This freeze, flight, or fight mechanism, as previously noted, requires no high-order cognitive processing; it is reactive and emotive (limbically). Our feet and legs not only react to threats and stressors, they are also reactive to our emotions, both negative *and* positive ones. The dancing and celebration we do today is an extension of the celebratory exuberance we exhibited millions of years ago upon the completion of a successful hunt. Around the world, it is the feet and legs that so often communicate happiness, whether it be Masai warriors jumping high in place or couples dancing up a storm. We even stomp our feet in unison at ball games to let our team know we are rooting for them.

Over the centuries, as our species developed vocal skills and language, the necessity to observe the feet became less important because we could call out danger at greater distances. Nevertheless, our feet remain one of the most important and truthful purveyors of our feelings and sentiments.

Proof of this statement abounds in our everyday life. You can see it in action for yourself. Note when two people (called a *dyad*) are talking in a hallway and are interested in having a private conversation, their feet will mirror each other and they will usually square off face-to-face. If someone should approach to join the dyad, they will be acknowledged in one of two ways by the feet. If the feet of the original two people remain fixed toward each other and only the upper torsos shift, then they really don't want the third person to join them. If, however, the feet of the two people open up to welcome the third person, then we can assume the third person is truly welcome. Most people will, at a minimum, turn the upper body toward the approaching person; that is done out of social grace. It is only when the feet move, to admit the new person, that the welcome is full and genuine.

You can also watch children and their foot movements for a real education. They may be sitting down to eat, but if they want to go out and play, notice how the feet sway, how they stretch to reach the floor even when they are not finished with their meal. The parent may try to hold them in place at the table, yet their feet will inch toward the door. Their torso may be held by that loving parent, but the children will twist and squirm their feet ever so diligently in the direction of the door—an accurate reflection of where they want to be. As adults, we are, of course, more restrained, but just barely so.

Those who dedicate their lives to decoding the world around them know that the feet, not the face, are the most accurate purveyors of sentiment. Having done thousands of FBI interviews, I learned to concentrate on the feet and the legs first, the hands and the face last. If you want to decode the world around you and interpret behavior accurately, watch the feet and the legs. They are truly remarkable and honest in the information they convey.

Happy Feet at the Poker Table

When it comes to reading body language, most poker players start at the top (face) and work their way down. My approach is the exact opposite: I begin with the feet and move up from there. This is because when it comes to the *honesty* of a person's responses, the degree of truthfulness decreases as we move from the soles of our feet to the top of our head. Thus, our feet are the most honest part of our body, and our face is the most deceptive.

When you think about it, there's good reason for the deceitful nature of our facial expressions. We lie with our face because that's what we've been taught to do since early childhood. "Don't make that face!" our parents growl when we honestly react to Aunt Wilma's treacherous meat loaf. "At least *look* happy when your cousins stop by," they add, and you learn how to force a smile. Mom and Dad are, in essence, telling us to hide, conceal, deceive, lie with our face . . . so we tend to get pretty good at it. So good, in fact, that when we put on a happy face at the poker table, we might look like we've got the mortal, stone-cold nuts when, in reality, we've got a seven-deuce offsuit and are in deep crapola.

Think about it: if we *couldn't* control our facial expressions, why would the term "poker face" have any meaning?

So I don't look for happy faces at the table, I look for what I call "happy feet"—feet that wiggle and/or bounce with joy at the table. Our feet are the most honest part of our body because we have never been taught to control them; and even if we had, it would be difficult to achieve, because the behavior is a limbic brain response that has been hardwired into our nervous system during an evolutionary period that spans millions of years.

A few months ago, I was watching a World Poker Tour final table on television. I see a guy dealt a flush and his feet are going wild! They are wiggling and bouncing like the feet of a child who's just learned he's going to Disney World. His face is stoic, his demeanor above the table is calm, but down near the floor there's a whole lot of shakin' goin' on! I'm pointing at the TV set and urging the other players to fold. Too bad they can't hear me. Two players call his bets to the river and lose to his flush.

This player has learned how to put on his best poker face. Obviously, he has a long way to go when it comes to putting on his best poker feet. Fortunately for him, his opponents hadn't read this book . . . and like most players, they have spent a lifetime missing three-fourths of the human body—from the chest on down—and paying no attention to what critical tells can be found there.

When players have happy feet, it's because they have great hands. It's a *high-confidence* tell, a signal that the player is strong and opponents should beware.

When I conduct poker seminars, the participants are always shocked when I talk about the importance of happy feet.

"You can't see the feet!" they argue.

That's not totally accurate. You can usually see the feet of the players on either side of you, and even if you can't, there's an easy way to determine if an opponent has happy feet. You need to look at his shirt and/or his shoulders: if his feet are wiggling or bouncing, his shirt and shoulders will be vibrating or moving up and down.

Try this little demonstration for yourself. Sit down in front of a full-length mirror and begin wiggling or bouncing your feet. What's going to happen is you'll start to see your shirt and/or shoulders move. If you're not watching for it, you might miss it; but if you're willing to look for shirt and shoulder movement, it can be readily detected in most cases.

When my poker seminar students see the vibrating shirt and shoulders of a player with happy feet, this is usually when the lightbulb goes off. They realize they've been missing an important tell at the tables and are quick to take advantage of it. Less than a month after the end of the first Camp Hellmuth, I received six e-mails from enrollees who reported significant gains in their bankrolls just by spotting happy feet in their opponents. Another participant from the camp saved himself from losing a huge pot when he decided not to call an opponent whose happy feet gave away the strength of his hand.

A word of caution: like all tells, happy feet must be taken in context to determine if they represent a true tell or just excess nervous behavior. For example, if a person has naturally jittery legs (a kind of restless-leg syndrome at the poker table), then it might be hard to distinguish happy feet from his normal nervous energy. If the rate or intensity of jiggling increased, however, particularly after a player saw his cards, I might view that as a potential signal that the strength of his hand had just taken a turn for the better.

Looking for an Under-the-Table Payoff Can Improve Your Poker Game!

Looking for tells that occur in the area between the top of the poker table and the floor can provide you with some interesting kickbacks in your game. Here are some other foot behaviors that can help you read your opponent at the tables (see figures 20–24).

1. *Watch for feet that turn away from the table.* We tend to turn away from things that we don't like or are disagreeable to us. Studies of courtroom behavior reveal that when jurors don't like a witness, they turn their feet toward the door from which they came. The same holds true for people who want to terminate a conversation. From the hips up, they will face the person they are talking with, but their feet will shift away, toward the nearest exit. If a player has kept her feet pointed forward during the early part of a hand and then, after seeing a later card (in

Fig.20. Feet flat on the ground.   **Fig.21. Feet suddenly rise, an intention cue.**

Hold'em, usually the flop, the turn, or the river) turns her feet away, it is normally a sign of disengagement, a signal that she no longer wants to be involved in the hand.

2. *If a person is constantly wiggling or bouncing his or her leg(s) and suddenly stops, pay attention.* This might be a sign that he or she is bluffing (a freeze response). Be attentive if the movement stops right after the player has placed a large bet, particularly if other freeze behaviors are in evidence (e.g., breath holding, overcontrol of other bodily movements).

3. *If a player's feet go from a resting position (flat) to a ready position—heel elevated, toes forward—this is an indication the person plans to act.* This is called an *intention cue* and suggests the person is going to

Fig. 22. Feet pigeon-toed—
indicative of insecurity or
discomfort.

Fig. 23. Interlocked ankles
may appear only when player
is bluffing.

get involved in the hand by calling, raising, or re-
raising.

4. *When a player suddenly turns his toes inward or inter-
   locks his feet, it is a sign that he is nervous and/or feels
   threatened.* Usually, this is an indication he has a marginal or weak hand. If, after making a bet, he wraps
   his feet around the legs of his chair, it's often a sign he's
   bluffing. He is unsure and is restraining himself.

5. *If you see a player push away from the table and cross
   her legs, one over the other, this is a* high-confidence
   tell and suggests that she has a good hand.

6. *When players make a big bet and then they interlock
   their ankles around the legs of their chair, this is a restraining (freeze behavior) that suggests they may be*

Fig. 24. Ankles wrapped suddenly around the chair legs is indicative of self restraint.

bluffing. They are constraining themselves because they fear they are going to be detected by their opponent as they bluff.

7. *Watch for the player who locks his feet around the chair and then moves his hand along his pants leg (like he is drying his hand on his trousers).* The feet lock is a freeze response and the hand rubbing is a pacifying behavior. The two, taken together, make it more likely that the player is bluffing. His body language is figuratively saying, "I'm really nervous here; please don't catch my bluff." (Note the hand-leg rub in figures 81 and 82, located on page 169).

8. *Players sometimes can be seen suddenly moving their feet from in front of their chairs to under their chairs.* This is normally a sign of weakness and/or bluffing behavior, especially when it follows action on the table, such as a flop.

Going Down to The-Feet So You Won't Go Down to De-feat

Because they are the most honest part of the body, the feet are most likely to provide the most accurate, uncensored information to the alert poker player. Here is a list of the various parts of a person's body, ranked in terms of honesty.

At the top of the list:

1. Feet (most honest)
2. Legs
3. Torso

4. Arms

5. Hands

6. Mouth

7. Eyes

At the bottom of the list: 8. Face (least honest)

In terms of tells, the feet will provide you with the most accurate information, while facial tells will give you the least accurate information. There is, then, a definite correlation between
the honesty of a specific part of the body and the accuracy of the
tell exhibited by that area of the body. In later chapters, I will
cover these other parts of the body that provide tells which, although not as accurate as the feet, are still valuable in reading
people and increasing your success at the tables.

Chapter 5

Tells of Engagement

Radar is a magnificent planning aid. By giving us advance notice of potential problems, it allows us more time and information to overcome those difficulties successfully. Could you imagine a major international airport without radar? I can assure you, it would be an air traffic controller's worst nightmare. Air traffic controllers need information about what's going on around them: they need to know where the pilots are and what they intend to do if air safety is to be maintained.

Wouldn't it be nice if we had radar at the poker table? Imagine how helpful it would be if you could get advance notice on where the players are in a hand and what they intend to do when it's their turn to act. That would certainly do wonders for your financial safety.

Well, the good news is that you *do* have a personal radar at the poker table . . . you just have to turn it on. This involves continual scanning of your opponents, knowing what tells to look for that provide advance notice of their intentions, and then using that information to play your own hand more effectively.

Intention Cues

Very early in my career as an FBI agent, I learned there were certain nonverbal tells to look for if you wanted to know what a person was *intending* to do before they did it. This was particularly helpful if the person was planning to do you bodily harm! A little advance notice can go a long way in avoiding serious injury or even death. One such nonverbal tell involved an individual's nose.

If you take your fingers and place them on either side of your nose, you can trace the contour of your nostrils. If you then sniffle, you can feel your nostrils expand. This is called a *nose flair,* or *naral wing dilation.* Nose flaring is a potent indicator that a person intends to do something physical. As the individual prepares to act, he will oxygenate, which causes the nose to expand. In my profession, if I see a suspect looking down (an act of concealment) and his nose is flaring, there's a high probability he's preparing to hit me. Knowing this information allows me to take appropriate defensive measures and keeps me from being sucker punched.

What about naral wing dilation at the poker table? Do we see it? Yes. Are we in physical danger? Not likely, unless it comes in the midst of an argument between players. At the poker table, nose flair is a tell of *intention* or *engagement:* it is letting us know that the player plans to get involved in the hand. This, of course, can be valuable information if you are thinking of coming into the pot and would like to know if anyone else intends to join you. I've been at a table where the last player to act was waiting for his turn to come around, and the whole time his nose was dilated. He couldn't wait to get his chips into the center of the table! If you were among the first players to act and were aware of this opponent's naral wing dilation, it might very well help you decide whether you should fold, call, or raise. Remember, nose flaring = action to follow.

There are other tells of intention that can also help you determine what players intend to do . . . before they do it. You should always be looking for signs of engagement versus disengagement in your opponents. What you will usually see is the player's torso leaning toward the table when he's going to engage in play, and away from the table when it doesn't suit him to get involved. One way to look at this behavior is in terms of energy. To expend the energy it takes to be in the forward/ready position actually taxes the body, which would much rather be relaxed and at ease. So when a person is in a relaxed position, leaning left or right, and suddenly shifts into the forward position, I see that as an *engagement tell,* as an *intention* to act.

Our hands are also a good source of engagement tells. When we're ready to join the action, we tend to move more of our hands onto the table. We also tend to fidget more because we're waiting for the action to come around for us. Fidgeting with chips is not a real good tell, because many people do this as a stress releaser. However, if you see players strumming their thumbs or wiggling them up and down, this is usually a sign of engagement, a gesture that says, "I'm impatient to make my bet." Conversely, if you see a player begin to withdraw her hands from the table as additional cards are dealt, or, perhaps, distance herself from her cards, her chips, and/or the table, you can assume that these are signs of disengagement—that, for some reason (probably a poor flop or

Fig.25. Feet poised suddenly in a runner's stance is highly indicative of intention.

other unfavorable card), she is planning to drop out of the hand. Again, knowing this information in advance of it actually happening can be very advantageous in helping you determine the best way to play your cards.

The position of our palms provides an interesting tell. Some players sit with their hands palm up, the so-called rogatory position (*rogatory* is Latin for "prayer"). This is *not* a ready position; a ready position is palms down. So if a player sits habitually with his palms up and all of a sudden—usually after seeing a card(s) for the first time—he puts his palms down, chances are he's getting ready to play his hand.

The position of a person's feet can be an accurate predictor of playing intentions. People who are getting ready to engage in play will shift their feet like a runner getting ready to go into the blocks; their heel(s) will go from being flat on the floor to a raised position, and their toes will be pointed forward (see figure 25).

Postural cues can also signal intentions to get involved in play. When a player who has been slouching or resting comfortably in her seat looks at her cards and suddenly snaps to attention and sits up straight in her chair, don't be surprised to see her get involved in the hand. What you're looking for is *changes* in sitting behavior. If someone is always sitting up straight and leaning slightly forward, it shouldn't be taken as an intention to engage; that is his normal posture, unlike the young lady who went suddenly from a slouch to an upright position. Now, if the person who always sat up straight and leaned slightly forward suddenly leaned back and away from the table, *that* might well be taken as an intention to not get involved—or end involvement—in the hand currently being played.

One of the classic tells of engagement—it's been discussed for decades—also reveals an individual's intention to participate

Fig.26. Player looks at cards
and immediately looks at
chips.

Fig.27. A quick look is indicative of intention and a good
hand.

in a hand, usually quite aggressively. It involves a player looking at his cards and then immediately (1) looking at his chips
and/or (2) reaching for his chips (see figures 26 and 27). One
would think that all the publicity surrounding this tell would
discourage the vast majority of players from displaying it, yet it
continues to be seen at the tables, reminding us once again that
it is difficult to disguise or eliminate behavior that has been
hardwired into us by our limbic brain.

Overprotection of the cards is another engagement tell.
When you see a player look at his cards and then "protect" them
or "get closer" to them, particularly when that behavior increases as additional cards are dealt, it is pretty certain that the
individual player will be an active participant in the hand (see
figure 28). Conversely, if the player suddenly distances himself

Fig.28. Overprotection of cards is sometimes seen
from an amateur holding a monster hand.

from his cards, or abandons them altogether, it is a strong indication that it won't take much for him to quit (or get bet out of) the game (see figures 29 and 30). The same holds true for chip behavior. Although many players toy with their chips, you should be alert to any opponent who suddenly protects or withdraws from his chips more than he has been doing when *not* involved in a hand. This is because sudden changes in chip-handling behavior can reflect the person's assessment of how well the hand is playing out from card to card.

One of the most interesting—and sometimes difficult to interpret—engagement tells involves the *pursing of the lips*. Take a moment, if you would, and purse your own lips as if you were going to kiss someone. People purse their lips when they are in disagreement with something or someone (see figure 31). When someone talks and we're not in agreement, we purse our lips. This is often seen during closing arguments in court trials. While one attorney speaks, opposing counsel will pursue their lips in disagreement. Judges also do it as they disagree with attorneys at sidebar conferences.

What about lip pursing at the poker table? If you watch a player and he purses his lips right after he has checked his hole cards or seen a community card, there's a good chance he's unhappy with what he's just seen and might very well disengage from the hand. This is particularly true if the lip pursing is accompanied by some other intention tell, like hand withdrawal from the table or a shift in the player's center of balance (see figure 32).

Here's an example of lip pursing I witnessed at a recent nine-handed cash game. A player had exhibited a high-confidence tell when he first looked at his hole cards and called a raise on the opening round of bets. When the flop came, how-

Fig.29. Player moves in close, thinking he has a good hand.

Fig.30. Turn card reveals he has a rag hand as he
subconsciously moves away.

Fig.31. Lip pursing takes place
when things don't go your way.

Fig.32. As things get worse,
the hands will withdraw as the
lips are further pursed.

ever, this same player pursed his lips. Another player put in a
large raise, and the lip-pursing individual threw his hand away. I
couldn't determine if his opponent had spotted the lip-pursuing
tell and taken advantage of it; however, watching for this kind of
tell suggests how valuable it can be when you're trying to put
someone on a hand.

There is, however, something additional to consider when
observing a pursed-lip response. As long as the pursed-lip behavior continues, it means the player is considering his alternatives.
The pursing behavior goes away once the decision is made. If you
play with the same opponent frequently and you are able to determine that he does this all the time (purses his lips until he makes
his decision), then you have a tremendous advantage. Now you
know that once the pursing is over, he's made his decision, so you

can immediately look for other tells that will suggest his plan of action. Does he withdraw his hands from the table? Does he lean forward? Does he reach for his chips? The more cues you put together, the more of the puzzle you can solve. What's important here is that you *know* when to start looking for the cues because you know that the moment the lip pursing stops, the player has made up his mind as to what he intends to do.

Watching for *engagement tells* can help you develop a better fight plan, just as an air traffic controller can watch his radarscope to develop a better flight plan. Use your personal radar to gain advance knowledge of what your opponents intend to do, and I suspect you'll be cleared for final-table play in no time at all. And remember, if you see an opponent across the table with his torso leaning forward, his arms on the table, his feet in a ready position, and his nostrils flaring, you should realize what he is about to do. Unless you have a super hand, fold!

Chapter 6

An Introduction to High- and Low-Confidence Tells

The next few chapters will describe some of the nonverbal behaviors players display when they have either high confidence or low confidence in their hands. I group these tells in several different categories to make them easier to understand and remember. None of these tells are 100 percent accurate for all players, and they should never be the only factor you consider in determining how to play your hand; however, judiciously integrated into your total playing strategy, they can be quite useful in helping you decide whether to fold, call, raise, or reraise your opponent(s).

Warning! You Can't Read Players Who Can't Read Their Hands

The tells I'll be describing in this chapter are *limbic brain behaviors;* therefore, they should honestly reflect a player's true intentions and beliefs. Problems arise when the player's true beliefs are wrong. This usually occurs with novice players who display high-confidence tells because they honestly believe they have a good hand when, in reality, they have a marginal or terrible hand. This is why playing against amateurs can be so frustrating for professional players. There can be four cards to a straight or a four flush on the board, and the inexperienced player is oblivious to this critical information. He is convinced his high pair in the hole is a great hand and gives off every high-confidence tell in the book, even though he's going to be a huge underdog in the showdown.

There is really nothing that can be done about these kinds of players, except to learn who they are as quickly as possible and remember they are unpredictable and oblivious to sophisticated ploys because they lack basic card wisdom and understanding of the game. Once you realize this type of person is at your table, just forget about reading him. It's not that he is lacking in tells; rather, his high-confidence tells are tainted by his ignorance that a pair of fives is not a mortal lock in a nine-handed game!

Some General Guidelines for Reading Tells Correctly

Reading tells is a skill that depends on effective observational techniques discussed in chapter 1. You'll need to know these techniques and employ them faithfully each time you play. I am not going to repeat them here, but I do want to highlight a few points you'll want to keep in mind as you observe your opponents at the tables.

1. *High-confidence tells are normally displayed by players who believe they have strong hands. Low-confidence tells are normally displayed by players who believe they have weak hands.*

2. *Not all tells at the table are related to poker.* I remember playing in a game in which an opponent across the table displayed a high-confidence tell before it was his turn to act. To my surprise, he folded his hand without even calling the bet. During a break, I overheard him talking to his wife. It turned out that his behavior was the result of winning a big sports bet. He had spotted the score scrolling across a TV monitor located near the table. Another time, I saw an individual clearly exhibit a low-confidence tell and then go all-in with pocket aces. Because I had never witnessed that type of tell with such strong cards, I congratulated him on his hand, hoping he might say something that would explain his behavior. As it turned out, his response was "It was a great hand; now, if I could just get over this migraine headache . . ." It was pain, not gain, that was responsible for the tell I observed. The best way to reduce the likelihood of misinterpreting tells like the two just described is to watch when they occur. If they happen immediately after a significant table event—for example, a player sees his hole cards for the first time or an opponent makes a big bet—chances are that the tells are related to the game in progress. If they occur when no specific or significant poker action is taking place, the probability increases that the cause of the tell is *not* related to the game in progress.

3. *Try to establish baseline behaviors for the players at your table.* You need to note how your opponents normally sit, their standard posture, where they place their hands, and their normal speaking behavior. That way you can determine when they deviate from their standard behaviors. For instance, if a person's hands shake when she looks at her cards or reaches for her chips, this is a high-confidence tell, an indication that player holds good cards. But if the player has natural hand tremors, this information will be useless. How do you know if this is the case? You need to get a baseline reading on the player's normal hand movements. One player at Camp Hellmuth was a habitual gum chewer. Every time he had a good hand, he would chew more rapidly. It was a powerful tell, but only to the observer who had noticed the habit, taken a baseline reading on the normal chewing rate, and was then in a position to notice the accelerated chewing rhythm when it occurred.

4. *Seek collaborating evidence whenever possible.* Because a person often responds to specific poker situations with multiple tells, you can always be more confident of your read if you can identify additional tells that are consistent with the one you have detected. If a player looks at her cards and displays *happy feet,* you can assume she has high confidence in her hand; if, at the same time, her eyes dilate, she executes an elevated chip toss when she bets, and then she leans back, interlacing her hands behind her head (all high-confidence tells), you can be 99.99 percent she has a great hand and the confidence to match.

5. *Track a player's tells over the entire course of each
    hand dealt. When an opponent shifts from a high-
    confidence to a low-confidence tell as new cards are
    revealed (or vice versa), this is particularly useful in-
    formation.* In one World Poker Tour event, a player
    checked her hole cards, moved her arms and body for-
    ward (high-confidence tells), and bet aggressively. Af-
    ter seeing the flop, however, she moved her arms and
    body away from the table (low-confidence tells). An-
    other player, possibly aware of her behavior, made a
    large bet and she folded. When a person's tells mirrors
    the changing strength of her hand, this is money in the
    bank for the alert observer.

**Fig.33. Steepled hands are
indicative of confidence.**

**Fig.34. The steeple may be
modified, as here, with fingers laced and only index
fingers up.**

Fig.35. Wringing of hands, especially where there is skin
blanching, is indicative of a poor hand.

6. *Watch for micro-gesture tells, those behaviors that oc-cur for a moment immediately after a significant table event.* If they are followed by secondary nonverbal behaviors that conflict with the initial reaction, then trust the micro-gesture tell, as it tends to be the more honest. An example here would be a person who, upon seeing his cards, steeples his fingers for a moment (high-confidence tell involving touching the spread fin-gertips from both hands together in an arched posi-tion) and then begins wringing his hands together (low-confidence tell). I would trust the high-confidence tell as the most honest and accurate (see figures 33–35).

7. *In general, tells of engagement (see chapter 5) tend to be related to greater hand strength, while pacifying behaviors (see chapter 12) tend to be associated with lower hand strength, bluffing, and/or unhappiness with specific actions at the table (bets, loss of a hand, dangerous chip or cash deficiency).*

8. *Observe your opponents and remember how they play. Their past behavior can be a helpful predictor of their future behavior.* As always, observed tells are most useful to you when (a) you are familiar with your opponent's play and know that a specific tell has been an accurate indicator of high or low confidence in the past; (b) after studying the behavior of an opponent you're facing for the first time, you determine that his confidence displays are, in fact, accurate indicators of his hand strength.

Chapter 7

High- and Low-Confidence Displays
Part I: Gravity-Defying Tells

Gravity-defying behaviors at the poker table are mostly high-confidence tells. They are the physiological equivalent of an *emotional exclamation point,* a sign of aroused excitement created when a player is looking at a strong hand. I call them gravity-defying tells because, when you think of them, they are usually pushing upward, against the force of gravity.

We tend to undertake gravity-defying behaviors, whether standing or sitting, when we are positive, excited, and energized by our current circumstances. Gravity-defying behaviors are rarely seen in people who are in trouble, afflicted, clinically depressed, or holding a lousy hand at the poker table. Gravity-defying behaviors are also governed by the limbic brain.

Can gravity-defying behaviors be faked? I suppose so, especially by really good actors and perennial liars, but in the end most people don't know how to moderate their limbic behaviors. Usually, what we see are more passive restrained behaviors rather than affirmative behaviors, and that is consistent with the abundance of research on gravity-defying behaviors that now exists.

Here are some of the gravity-defying behaviors that can bring you some down-to-Earth profits at the poker table.

A Rise in the Feet Means the Cards Held Are Sweet

When we are happy and excited, we walk as if floating on air. We see this with young lovers excited to be around each other, in children who are eager to enter a theme park, and poker players holding strong hands.

Gravity-defying behaviors, especially ones involving our feet, are part of our emotive expressions. When we are excited about our hand—when we feel positive about the cards we are holding—we tend to defy gravity by doing such things as *raising our heels* and/or *bouncing our feet and legs*. As stated before, this is the limbic brain, once again, manifesting itself with *happy feet*.

We discussed the importance of foot tells in chapter 4, so I won't dwell further on them here, except to remind you that the happy-feet response is one of the most honest and accurate tells for determining the strength of your opponent's cards.

When You See a High Chin, Someone Thinks He Can Win

Players who hold their chin higher than they normally do are displaying a high-confidence tell. Because the chin is held up, it is a

Fig.36. A high chin at the table is suggestive
of a great hand.

gravity-defying gesture, and a sign of positive news at the poker table (see figure 36). On the other hand, when the cards aren't looking too good, expect the player to keep his chin down.

Have you ever heard the old adage "Keep your chin up"? It's a remark directed at someone who is in the doldrums or experiencing misfortune (a bad poker hand, perhaps?). This bit of folk wisdom accurately mirrors the tells we are discussing here, as a person with his chin down is not in good shape, while a person with his chin up is perceived as being in good shape and in a positive frame of mind.

A Nose in the Air Means Good Cards Are There

Again, we have a gravity-defying gesture (nose *up*) indicating a high-confidence tell, while a nose-down position would indicate a low-confidence display. When a player's nose goes high, it's because he's confident of what he has. Many years ago, an interesting experiment was conducted that speaks to this behavior. A group of students who smoked cigarettes were observed to see if they had passed or failed an exam in school after receiving their results. Those students who had done well exhaled their cigarette smoke *upward,* while those who had performed poorly exhaled *downward*. Although smoking is relatively rare at poker tables these days, if you should run across a smoker who looks at his cards and exhales up, you might want to think twice about coming over the top of him.

Fig.37. Players arch their eyebrows when they like something, like a good hand.

The Eyebrow Arch: Think Groucho Marx

I don't know how many of you remember the Marx Brothers. They were a comedy team, and Groucho always got a laugh by arching his eyebrows whenever he saw a beautiful woman. Well, it's not a laughing matter for poker players who reveal the strength of their hand by arching their eyebrows whenever they see a beautiful hand (see figure 37). But some of them do, and this is another gravity-defying high-confidence tell. You might have the last laugh, however, if you spot the behavior and use it to your advantage at the tables. If you'll recall, that's exactly what Phil did at his first poker camp when he spotted an opponent display an eyebrow arch and immediately folded, saving himself a bundle of money in the process.

Sitting Erect = Good Cards from the Deck

Poker players who see cards that give them powerful hands tend to raise their posture and their bets: they sit more erect, almost seeming to grow in height. Once again, they are displaying a gravity-defying gesture that is a high-confidence tell (see figure 38). When you see this sudden display of erect posture (particularly after a player has just seen his or her cards), you might want to consider shrinking the size of your bets.

Taking a "Stand" Can Mean a Good Hand

Some players get so excited when they get a strong hand that they literally cannot contain their limbic arousal response and

Fig.38. Sitting up suddenly at the table is a high-confidence display.

simply stand up, thus displaying the most pronounced gravity-defying behavior in the world of poker. It's almost as if there's a pressure cooker on a high flame that's going to explode if something isn't done. I have seen many amateur players stand up because they just can't deal with their emotions sitting down. I have watched some players literally leap from their chair and move way from the table because their excitement was so high (see figure 39). This standing behavior can best be identified as a high-confidence tell when it is displayed in conjunction with other behaviors consistent with a person holding a strong hand.

Standing at the table is not always a result of high-confidence behavior. During long playing sessions, some players will periodically stand during a hand to stretch their legs. Players will also stand when they are all-in on a hand and face the possibility of having to leave the game should they lose. I also notice that players stand when a pot is being contested on the last card and/or when an opponent stands up first. Thus, standing behavior is one of the weaker tells when it comes to determining high confidence and hand strength in an opponent.

An Elevated Chip Toss Could Reduce Your Chip Loss

The last gravity-defying behavior I'd like you to consider as a high-confidence tell involves the manner in which players put their bets into the pot. There are many ways this can be done: the chips can be pushed in, dropped in, even tossed in on a trajectory that is level with the tabletop. But there's only one chip placement I've discovered that has the potential to reveal a player's hand strength.

Fig.39. Some players will leap up with positive excitement when they see a good card that can help them turn their hand into a winner. Why, then, is this player standing? Did you note he was losing the hand from what you can observe in the picture? If you did, then you're already developing the observational skills necessary to read 'em and reap! (Many readers will just glance at the photo and not notice the discrepancy between what they're seeing and how the player is behaving. We hope you did!) What the picture doesn't show is the turn card, a king, which the dealer has just placed face-up beyond the border of the photo but easily spotted by the excited player. He is standing up, alert to the realization that he now holds trip kings against his opponent's full house, giving him a better chance (7 new outs) of winning the hand on the river.

Fig.40. An arched chip toss is indicative of high confidence.

I've noticed that when players have real good hands, they will arch their chips up and into the middle of the table, a kind of "rainbow toss" that occurs with a pot they think they can win at the end of that rainbow (see figure 40). Be wary when you see a player arch his chips into the pot with an elevated toss; it is often a sign that the bettor has a strong hand you might not want to challenge.

Lift-Off With a Pocket Rocket and Board Companion: An Ace Brings on a Gravity-Defying Tell

A gravity-defying tell helped me predict that Kevin McBride held an ace in the hole when he played Scotty Nguyen for a large pot in the 1998 World Series of Poker. After both players had bet their hole cards, the flop came 4-6-K. Then, on fourth street, an ace was dealt and Kevin made a small, nearly imperceptible "jump" in his chair. I therefore assumed that the ace on the board had helped his hand, which meant it probably paired one or both of his hole cards. The river card was a queen. Sure enough, when the cards were turned over, Kevin showed a pocket ace and queen.

Chapter 8

High- and Low-Confidence Displays
Part II: Territorial Tells

Most territorial tells are revealed in two kinds of distancing behaviors: near-far and expansion-contraction.

The Near-Far Dimension

In general, any player deviation from his baseline behavior that brings him closer to the center point of the table is a high-confidence display. Any deviation from his baseline behavior that adds greater separation between the player and the center point of the table is a low-confidence display.

If you think about the social interactions you've had in your life, you'll realize that we lean toward people we like and away from those individuals we dislike. The same is true at the poker table: you'll see somebody check her hole cards and suddenly she'll draw nearer to the table. Why? Because she has a great hand. Her limbic brain is saying, "You're happy," and one way we reflect happiness is by drawing near to the object/person that is causing it. I've seen this behavior thousands of times at the tables, yet many players dismiss the importance of this distancing tell by assuming it's just an opponent "adjusting her seat." Don't *you* be one of those players!

Sometimes you'll see a player start a new game with her hands resting on the rim of the table. Then, after seeing her hole cards, she'll move her hands slightly onto the green baize layout. Comes the flop, and she moves her hands slightly forward again. By fifth street, her hands are on the green felt up to the elbows! Each new card has improved her hand, and has seduced her to move ever nearer to the center of her attraction. If you're still betting with this woman at the river, you better have a *very* strong hand!

Here's another thing you'll notice about players' hands. When we like things, we put our hands closer to them; when we don't, we move our hands away. At a recent tournament, a player was playing with his chips, separating and joining them together between his fingers. All of a sudden, he saw the flop and moved his hands away from his chips. His limbic brain was saying, "That's bad," and he behaved in a predictable manner: he removed himself from the area where the bad event was centered. At a different tournament, a player was cupping his hands over his cards, protecting them like a mother cat wrapped around her kittens. A flop with three diamonds hit the felt, and the player lifted his hands from the cards and onto the rail. When the dealer turned up another diamond on the turn, the player completely removed his hands from the table, folding them in his lap. As his hand went from good to bad, his hands went from near to far. Once again, we see the tendency for individuals to

**Fig.41. Interlacing of fingers behind the head
is a high-confidence display.**

approach the positives and retreat from the negatives in their
lives, whether it be people they know or the cards in their
hands.

There is one important exception to this near-far dimension
in territorial tells. This is when a player pushes or leans away
from the table (normally a *low*-confidence display of disengagement), but combines this movement with a high-confidence flour-
ish: usually crossing his legs and/or interlacing his fingers behind
his head (see figure 41). I have never seen a person with a poor
hand lean back and put his hands behind his head! This behavior
is reserved for players with "boss" hands or bosses sitting domi-
nantly at a meeting with their subordinates.

There are times when these tells are so outlandish one would
think they were intentionally faked. At Camp Hellmuth, I was
watching a player from *six* tables away. When the flop was dealt,

he checked his cards, took a swig of his beer, leaned back in his chair, and rested his hands behind his head. Nobody at the table paid any attention to his behavior. They were calling and raising as if nothing unusual was happening. He took another swig of beer and maintained his position throughout the balance of the hand. In the end, he turned up the nuts, four jacks. I kept asking myself, "Why are his opponents still playing?" How could they be unaware of this high-confidence display that I could readily see six tables away? Then it dawned on me: none of the players understood the *significance* of his behavior. They *saw* the behavior, but they didn't *decipher* it correctly.

That's why I wrote this book!

The Expansion-Contraction Dimension

In general, any deviation from a player's normal baseline behavior that widens her territorial boundaries is a high-confidence display; any deviation from her baseline behavior that narrows her territorial boundaries is a low-confidence display.

When I think of territorial expansion, I'm always reminded of the image of a proud parent puffing out his or her chest. At the poker table, players with high confidence are going to expand themselves physically as well as geographically. Players with good cards "extend out." Their legs spread out under the table, their arms stretch out over the table, their elbows flair further from their torso (elbow flair), their shoulders broaden, and they literally take over a larger portion of the table, like a driver hogging the road. Sometimes players will actually gain territory by tilting their head to one side or the other. This is a high-comfort, high-confidence display. I seriously doubt you can have a bad

Fig. 42. A pious, withdrawn look is indicative of low confidence.

hand and maintain a head-tilt behavior. (If you see an opponent with his head tilted after viewing his hole cards and suddenly, after seeing the flop, his neck straightens up and his head goes erect, you can suspect that those three community cards were not bearers of good news!)

Because territorial dominance is hardwired within our limbic systems, we rarely see it except when someone has supreme confidence in his hand. This is *not* the kind of person you'll likely bluff out of a pot.

Then there's territorial contraction, which, in many ways, is the mirror opposite of the expansive behavior just described. Players who exhibit low-confidence contraction tells at the table shrink their territorial and physical boundaries (see figure 42). One world champion poker player described these individuals as literally "wilting at the table." When players have low confidence in their cards, they'll draw their elbows and arms in and look almost pious. One major player on the World Poker Tour circuit has a strong territorial contraction tell. As soon as he has a poor hand, he almost goes into an embryonic position. I can't tell you who it is because that would be unethical, but I'm always amazed that he can display this behavior time and time again without being found out by his opponents.

Chapter 9

High- and Low-Confidence Displays
Part III: Tells of the Hands

Our hands are an intimate part of poker. Not only do they provide the closest contact with our opponents, they also reach for and manipulate the two most important items on the table: the cards and the chips. To the conscientious observer, they also reveal tells that can be used to gain an advantage over the other players. Some of these tells have been discussed previously; the new ones are included in this chapter.

The Hand Steeple: A Powerful High-Confidence Tell

Hand steepling may very well be the most powerful high-confidence tell one can observe at the poker table. It involves touching the spread fingertips from both hands together in an arched position, a position similar to praying, but the fingers

Fig.43. Look for a "flash" steeple that occurs quickly after a flop—it's a good indicator of a monster hand.

are *not* interlocked (see figure 43). In the United States, women tend to steeple low, which sometimes makes it hard to see (men tend to steeple higher then women). Nevertheless, it is a nonverbal behavior well worth watching for. I have seen literally hundreds of players—amateur and professional—telegraph their card strength through steepling, even those who were aware of the tell but still had difficulty concealing it. This is because the limbic brain has made it such an automatic response that it is difficult to overcome, particularly when the excitement of seeing a good hand makes a player momentarily forget to monitor and control his or her behavioral reactions.

For players who are unaware their steepling is a tell, the response can persist for significant periods of time during a hand, particularly if the hand remains strong as new cards are revealed.

For players who *are* aware of the steepling tell but still display it, here's what you can expect to see. *Immediately* after observing a card (or cards) that makes them a strong hand, the player will perform the steeple as a *micro-gesture*. It is a pure limbic response; automatic, free of any "thinking" restraints. (In a metaphorical sense, think of the steepling as the flash of lightning right before the thunder.) Then, as the neocortex kicks in (the thunder) and the player realizes he has revealed this tell, he quickly moves his hands into a more neutral position, perhaps rubbing his hands together, to avoid detection by his opponents.

In a recent World Series of Poker match, a player held pocket aces and a third ace fell on the flop. When the player first saw the flop, he immediately steepled, and then, right afterward, he cupped his hands together and continued to play. This was a classic case of attempted deception: getting caught with your hand in the cookie jar and then trying to feign innocence by reaching for the drinking glass immediately beside it. In the case of the WSOP player, you can have confidence that the steeple reaction was an honest response to his cards because (a) it was quick, (b) it was in direct response to the "good news" presented by the flop, and (c) it was followed by an attempted act of concealment (the rapid transition from steeple to cupped hands).

You might recall that during the discussion of observation in chapter 1, I emphasized that any micro-gesture tends to be more reliable because it's more honest: the limbic brain recognizes it and causes a "true" response before the neocortex (thinking brain) takes over and censors (eliminates or modifies) the response.

One final note on hand-steepling behavior: some people have a habit of steepling; it is a way they normally hold their hands and is not necessarily a reaction to a highly favorable stimulus. You will need to study your opponents to learn if this

Fig.44. A steeple followed by hand-wringing can be
indicative of low confidence.

is the case. Again, it's a matter of establishing baseline criteria for specific behaviors so you'll know if and when they are significant tells. This is not as hard as it sounds. It is relatively easy to distinguish between players who steeple only after significant events occur at the table and those who randomly exhibit the behavior at various times during play and between hands.

Hand-Wringing and Interlacing Fingers: Low-Confidence Tells

A hand steeple can provide you with a high-confidence tell when you're trying to assess your opponent's hand strength. But what about the other end of the continuum: are there hand behaviors that can be construed as a low-confidence tells? Yes, there are. When players *wring their hands together or interlace their fingers,* particularly in response to a significant event at the table, these are low-confidence behaviors that suggest they hold weak cards (see figure 44).

Hands That Shake: Your Chips Are at Stake—Usually

Our limbic system is not called the emotional brain for nothing. When it sees or senses something desirable and exciting (like pocket aces), the arousal level goes up, and you can see in the affected person—to quote the old song—"a whole lot of shakin' going on!" This nonverbal behavior is often misinterpreted by individuals who observe it. This is because most people believe that bad things are happening to people if their hands are shaking and/or they are making erratic movements. But in poker, at least, the opposite is true. When you see someone reaching for his chips and his shaking hand knocks them over, or he looks at his cards and his hands begin to tremble, it's usually a strong sign that something good has occurred, like Big Slick (AK) or a high pair in the hole.

This is your limbic system saying, "I'm happy," and so your hands vibrate. And if this vibration doesn't show in the hands, it'll show elsewhere, like in your wiggling feet. Thus, erratic movements and shaking hands are high-confidence tells that suggest your opponent holds strong cards. This is particularly true of amateur players, who have not learned to tone down their exuberance when sitting on a strong hand, and in almost all players when truly large amounts of money are at stake.

But wait . . . before you attribute *all* erratic, shaky behavior to good hands, I have to present a caveat: our hands can shake when we're excited, but it's also possible that they can shake when we're under stress (like when we have a weak hand and are trying to bluff). So, how can one tell the difference? Once again, the only way to accomplish this is to put the tell in the *context* of the game; consider the circumstances in which it occurred.

Let's dissect a typical hand and see what we can discover. Assume we're observing an opponent as he looks at his hole cards and his hands are steady, but upon seeing the flop his hands begin to shake. I'd assume he has a great hand. Now, let's examine the same situation, but this time the player's hands don't shake upon seeing the flop, but they do when he makes a big bet after the flop. This time I might assume the shaking is due to the stress involved with a bluff. If the bet is also accompanied by other pacifying tells, like touching the neck or a lip press, I'd be even more confident that the shaking was related to stress (rather than high confidence). Obviously, if the player's hands were shaking both after he saw his cards *and* when he bet, I'd assume his hand was good and his confidence was high.

In general, hand shaking that begins or increases immediately after a player sees a new card (or cards) is usually a sign of card strength and high confidence. Hand shaking that begins immediately after other significant table events take place—usually involving betting by the shaky player or his/her opponents—is more likely to be the result of stress. Even here, however, there can be exceptions to the rule. For example, say a player has been dealt pocket aces in early position and decides to limp into the pot. Her hands don't begin shaking when she looks at her cards, but rather when she puts her minimum bet into the pot. Here, with little money at stake, is a case in which I might suspect the shaking is due to a good hand and not a stressful and/or large bet. Of course, I'd try to spot other tells that would help me verify the accuracy of my assumption. In the meantime, I definitely wouldn't raise her hand in these circumstances, until I got a better read on the behavior.

As is the case in all attempts to determine tells, you need to have a baseline reading on your opponents' normal hand steadiness so you can note when significant changes in movement occurs. There are very few players out there who tremble all the way through a poker session, but there are individual differences in physical arousal that need to be taken into account when assessing the true meaning of erratic movements and/or shaking hands. Any shaking behavior that starts or stops suddenly, or is markedly different from baseline behavior, deserves further scrutiny. Considering the context in which the shaking occurs, when it occurs, and any other tells that might support a specific interpretation of why it's happening will improve your ability to read a person correctly.

A Chip off the Old Clock

The hand might not be quicker than the eye, but it can move pretty fast when it comes to reaching for chips for betting purposes. The question is, how fast does a player reach for his chips once he has seen his cards and is ready to bet? It turns out that the more rapidly individuals reach for their chips after seeing their card(s), the more likely it is they have a strong hand. Amateurs are more likely to exhibit this tell, as more seasoned players don't normally make such obvious moves. This tell, if present, is most effectively seen when a player must bet immediately after seeing her cards; in other words, when she is first to act (under the gun). Otherwise, by the time the betting action gets around to other players, the immediate need to reach for chips is no longer an issue.

A more subtle tell, and one that can be used with players even when they're not under the gun, involves *any* movement of a player's hand toward his chips immediately after seeing one or more new cards for the first time. Getting a baseline behavior will be important here, but if a player normally doesn't move his hand toward his chips except when he bets, you can begin to have confidence that the behavior does represent a high-confidence tell.

Fig.45. Thumbs-up displays
such as this indicate a very
confident player.

Fig.46. If thumbs disappear
into the pockets or the waistband, it is indicative of a weak
hand.

Two Thumbs Up: A Poker Hand
Just Got a Good Review

When somebody gives the thumbs-up sign, it usually means
something good just happened, and that holds true at the poker
table, too. Have you ever noticed how attorneys or doctors grab
their jacket lapels with their thumbs up? This is a high-confidence
display. At the poker table, the high-confidence thumb displays
are different, but no less significant. One high-confidence sign
involves the interlacing of the fingers (normally a *low-confidence*
tell) with the two thumbs sticking straight up (see figure 45). You
can see this tell two or three tables away. It is saying, "I've got a
good hand!" Normally, people don't sit with their thumbs up, so

when they do, one can be relatively certain that this is a significant behavior to consider in deciding your next poker move.

Twiddling the thumbs is another hand movement that indicates high confidence. What about low-confidence thumb tells? Players who stick their thumbs in their pockets or otherwise make their thumbs disappear by placing them inside their waistband may be demonstrating low-confidence tells (see figure 46). Again, baseline thumb behavior is important to ascertain. Normally, people leave their thumbs in a neutral position, neither up nor down. Therefore, thumb elevation and/or disappearing thumbs (thumb deflation) deserve your careful consideration.

Chapter 10

High- and Low-Confidence Displays
Part IV: Tells of the Mouth

In chapter 4, I noted that our feet are the most honest part of our body in that they reflect our true sentiments very accurately. Our face, in contrast, is the least honest, even though it is the most expressive portion of our anatomy. This means we must be very cautious when making inferences based on facial cues, as deceptive behavior is a very real possibility. Keep in mind that people often work at hiding their emotions and expressions, making it more difficult to read them if we are not attuned to carefully observe. For example, we certainly don't want to show elation when dealt a winning hand in poker. So we will try to conceal our happiness and excitement in these circumstances. Also, our facial cues are so fleeting—just quick micro-gestures—that they are difficult to pick up. Finally, facial cues often go unnoticed because we have been taught not to stare or because we concentrate too much on *what* is being said, rather than on *how* it is being said. These cautionary notes sounded, there are still some relatively reliable and noteworthy tells one can glean from observing certain *parts* of the face, the first area of interest being the mouth.

A False Smile and a Real Tell

For over a century, scientists have known that we humans have both a fake and a real smile. The fake smile is used socially when we don't really feel an emotional closeness to those around us; the real smile is reserved for those we truly care about. In fact, babies several weeks old will already reserve the real smile for their mothers and utilize the fake smile for all others.

Over time, researchers discovered that a true smile shows on the face because of two significant muscles, the *zygomatic majoris* and the *orbicularis oculi* (near the eyes), both working together to draw the corners of the mouth up and toward the eyes, causing "crow's-feet." This causes the familiar warm, honest smile (see figure 47).

When we have a false smile, the lip corners stretch sideways through the use of one set of muscles called the *risorious*. This muscle effectively pulls the corner of the mouth sideways but cannot lift it upward, as is the case with a true smile (see figure 48).

Real smiles are difficult to fake when we feel negative emotions. Case in point: if you are unhappy, according to researchers, it is unlikely that you will be able to smile fully (the true smile) using both the *zygomatic majoris* and the *orbicularis oculi* muscles. This brings us to fake smiles, true smiles, and the poker table.

Here's a classic tell I see frequently repeated wherever poker hands are contested. One player at the table is bluffing and an

Fig.47. Note that a real smile
involves the corner of the
eye—an honest display.

Fig.48. False smiles pull lips
toward ears—low confidence
and dishonesty are at play.

opponent challenges him with a comment like "What do you
have there? I'll bet it's no better than a seven and a king." The
bluffer now tries to create an impression that the opponent is
wrong, that he has a strong hand and isn't on a bluff. He does
this by flashing a smile that is supposed to indicate strength, but
it is the partial, false smile, not the honest, full smile. Recall that
it is difficult to give a full smile when you're unhappy, so you can
assume that this bluffer, fearful that his deception might be discovered, is probably most unhappy at this particular moment!
When a player displays the false smile, it is normally very brief;
but to a trained observer, it is easy to detect and recognize for
what it is—an affirmation that a bluff is in progress. When
someone really does have a good hand, he responds to his opponent's verbal probe with an expressive, full smile.

The false-smile tell just described is yet another reminder of why I recommend not communicating with others at the table, particularly during the play of a hand. If a player asks you a question about the strength of your cards, just ignore him. Don't shrug, don't smile, don't reply verbally—just retain your "conceal, don't reveal" table posture and let the game continue. You may not be deemed very sociable, but your play will probably be far more profitable.

Lips That Are Pressed Means the Person Is Stressed; Lips That Are Full Signals Good Hand, No Bull!

Lip compression—also known as pressed or disappearing lips—occurs when a person is angry, grieving, frustrated, or dismayed. What happens is that we press our lips together, a limbic brain command that tells us to shut down and not allow anything into our body. Lip compression is very indicative of true negative sentiments that manifest quite vividly in real time. It rarely, if ever, has a positive connotation.

Lip compression is a clear sign that people are troubled. Something is wrong. At the poker table, lip compression serves as an indication that a person disapproves of something taking place during the play of a hand (see figure 49). If, after glancing at her hole cards, a player does a quick lip press, you can be sure that something is not good, because that's the only time we use a lip press. Thus, it is probably fair to assume the player has a weak hand.

Or consider this example. A player makes a bet and an opponent comes over the top of him with a raise. Upon seeing the

Fig. 49. Lip compression is highly indicative of stress and low confidence.

Fig. 50. Lip withdrawal is indicative of stress setting in.

raise, the player performs a lip press. Again, we can assume this is *not* something he wanted to have happen. He's disappointed it took place. The question becomes, *why* was he disappointed? Was it because he was bluffing and now he's in trouble? Or perhaps he expected to steal the blinds and didn't figure he'd be challenged. Maybe he's unhappy because calling the raise would cost him more than he wanted to invest in the hand. What we know for sure is that the raise troubled the player, so we need to look for other tells and/or the cards dealt to try to figure out why he is so stressed.

Most of the time when we see opponents with disappearing lips, it bodes well for us, particularly if the tell occurs right after they saw any new cards (see figure 50).

When *we* need to worry is when we look across at an opponent and see *full*—rather than compressed—lips. This is

Fig.51. Keep an eye on the
lips as indicators of
stress—normal lips.

Fig.52. Nail biting is a low-
confidence display.

because when things are going well, the lips "come out." The
limbic brain is saying, "Fill the lips with blood." You should be
particularly cautious if you see a player go from a lip press to a
full lip display (see figure 51). Something has just happened to
make the player feel a whole lot better—make sure it's not your
chips in his pile at the end of the hand.

Nailing Down Some Tells of the Lips, Tongue, and Teeth

What kind of hand do you think a person has if, while waiting to
see what the other players intend to do, he bites his nails? Here's a
hint: nail biting is an indication of stress (see figure 52). And the

Fig.53. Lip biting is a good indicator of stress and concern.

Fig.54. Nose touching takes place when we pacify to deal with a stressor.

Fig.55. Mouth touching is a good way to relieve the stress caused by a rag hand.

answer is . . . when I see someone biting their nails at the table, even when it's just for a moment, they've got a weak to mediocre hand. I have yet to see a person with a strong hand engage in such behavior.

This nail-biting tell will not be as useful, of course, with people who have a habit of chewing at their fingers; however, even these individuals should be considered candidates for further scrutiny should the intensity and/or frequency of their nail biting suddenly spike from their normal baseline behavior.

When players display other mouth signs associated with stress such as lip biting, mouth or nose touching, lip licking, or object biting, it further bolsters a careful observer's belief that the player has low confidence in his hand, which is most likely mediocre/marginal at best (see figures 53–57). When players

Fig.56. Lip licking takes place to pacify us when we are concerned.

Fig.57. Biting of objects— whether a finger or a pencil— is used to pacify our concerns or fears.

touch and/or lick their lips while pondering their options, particularly when they take an unusual amount of time to make a betting decision when it's their turn to act, they are usually trying to decide if playing their marginal hand is worth the risk. Oftentimes, they are vulnerable to bold play by their opponents and will usually fold against an aggressive raise.

The Way You Speak "Tells" If You're Strong or You're Weak

Some of you might be wondering why I'm including a discussion of speech in a book on nonverbal behavioral tells. It is because nonverbal behavior encompasses *how* you say things—for example, the rate, timbre, fluidity, and amplitude of speech. What you say is not of concern.

Scientific studies have concluded that your communication will be *fluid* if you have high confidence. Low confidence, on the other hand, is marked by broken speech or verbal behavior that is more high-pitched or slower (phlegmatic) than normal. Earlier in the book, I mentioned how Phil Hellmuth determined an opponent was bluffing by asking him a question and then listening to the man's voice as he replied. You can use this questioning approach to detect tells in an opponent. Not every opponent will answer you, and of those that do, not every person will reveal a tell. But it does provide an additional way to try to get a line on your opponents' intentions and quality of the cards they are holding. Just remember not to be a *giver* of such information by answering other players' questions, thereby possibly revealing critical information about your own hand and playing strategy. Along these lines, remember to keep your chips neatly stacked by color and easily viewed so that if someone asks you for a chip count, you can give a succinct answer without having to use your hands (a simple glance at your stack should suffice) or unnecessary verbal counting, either of which might provide your opponents with tells you don't want them to have.

The One Universal Sign Someone Got Away with Something!

In this, my final example of a mouth tell, I'd like you to participate in a small demonstration. First, I'd like you to lick your lips. This is called a *pacifying* behavior (to be discussed in chapter 12)

Fig.58. Tongue jut is a good indicator that someone just got away with something.

and is normally undertaken when a person is under stress. We also do it when we are concentrating on something, particularly a tasty dinner at a fine restaurant! Now I want you to protrude your tongue from between your teeth *without* touching your lips. It's a very quick movement—the tongue goes out between the teeth and comes back in a fraction of a second, almost like a snake flicking its tongue. I hope you can feel the difference between the two behaviors (see figure 58).

I call this second behavior a *tongue jut*. In my travels throughout the world, I have seen it used in many different countries, but always with the same meaning: "I got away with something!"

Once you learn to spot this behavior, it can be very helpful in any situation in which bargaining or competition is involved. Let me give you a personal example to prove my point.

Several years ago, I was shopping for a car in Tampa, where I live. I went to the dealership and told the salesman, "Here is what I am willing to pay for the car." We haggled over the price for a while, and finally the salesman did one of those "Well, let me clear it with my manager" routines. He left to find the manager, and I stepped outside his office to walk around and stretch my legs. A few minutes later, I happened to catch a glimpse of my salesman and his manager talking with each other behind a glass partition. I couldn't hear what they were saying, but I could see them clearly . . . and what I saw was the salesman give a quick, but unmistakable, tongue jut as he finished speaking to the manager before heading back to speak with me.

I went back to the salesman's office and waited for him to return. It didn't take him long. He popped in the door and said, "My manager agrees that the deal I offered you is the best we can do."

I asked, "So you're saying that's the best deal you can offer?"

"Yes," he replied.

"And that's *final*," I said in a let's-be-clear-about-this tone of voice.

"Yeah," he nodded. "That's our best price."

"OK, then, thank you," I announced. I got up from my chair, walked out of the office, and headed toward the front door. As I reached the exit, I heard my name and the words "Wait! Wait!"

The salesman coaxed me back into his office and informed me that he could take another $1,700 off their so-called best price offer—which, by the way, was only $86 more than I wanted to pay for the car in the first place. The moral to the story? It pays to know the bottom-line price you should be paying on a car—and also that when you see a tongue jut by your salesman, you know he's trying to get away with something!

Watching for tongue juts at the table can be very important, because when you see one, you gain important information. For example, imagine that a player under the gun (first to act) limps in with a monster hand, hoping to lure others into betting or raising, thus building a pot while enabling her to keep her hand strength disguised and/or providing the opportunity to come in over the top of the raiser. Immediately after she limps in, the person next to her (or one of two positions away) calls or raises the bet and she does a tongue jut. If you're one of the last players to declare and see her behavior, you know she thinks she got away with something. It's probably time you got away from something, too . . . *your hand!*

Here's another way spotting a tongue jut can be of value to you. Let's say that a player comes over the top of you on a raise and you're forced to fold your cards. As he pulls in the chips, you notice he does a tongue jut. What good is that? He already has your money. That is true, but you have just learned that he feels he got away with something, so you can assume he bluffed you out of the pot. That is information that might save or earn you money in a later hand, particularly if you now carefully watch his table behavior for signs of a bluff the next time you go up against him on a hand.

Tongue juts can be useful tells when you're playing in satellites, where deals are often made between players before the tournament is over. A typical example might involve a situation where you're one of three players left in a one-table satellite. Someone suggests a deal. You tentatively agree to the offer by saying, "I think that might work," and then watch the other two players for any tongue-jut tells. If you see one, you can quickly add, "On second thought, I don't feel comfortable with the way we're splitting the pot," and come up with your own suggestion.

Finally, remember that tongue-jut tells can be valuable whenever you see them at the table, even when you're not involved in the hand. This is because a tongue jut reveals a great deal about players and the various strategies they use and the risks they take in trying to win hands. Armed with this information, you might be the one that's next in line to do our own tongue jut.

Just don't do it where it can be seen!

The Professor's Talking Tell

Joe is 100 percent correct when he speaks of how a person's speech can reveal powerful tells to the sophisticated listener. That is why I like to get people talking when we're contesting a hand. For example, when someone makes a big bet against me, I ask right off: "How many chips do you have left?" That forces them to look at how many chips they have, or they tell me, or they're forced to count the chips or make other movements with their hands or body. Getting opponents to move and speak gives me a better chance to spot tells that reveal the relative strength or weakness of their hand. One classic example of this "get 'em to talk" strategy played out during the $5,000 buy-in Hall of Fame No-Limit Hold'em Championship in 2002.

With the blinds at $50–$100, the following hand came up. I limped under the gun (I called $100 as first player to act) with Kh-8h, and Howard ("The Professor") Lederer called right behind me, and then a couple of other players called as well. The flop came down Kd-8d-3h, and I was thinking, "Yippee, I have the top two pair!" I bet out $400, and Howard called me; then another player moved all-in for $775 total. When the other two players in the pot folded, I quickly decided two things: first, I wasn't sure that I could legally raise, since my bet was $400 and the raise was only $375 more, but I thought I could; second, I didn't want to ask if I could raise and let Howard know the real strength of my hand. So immediately, when it was my turn to act, I just called the $375 raise, trying to look weak and disinterested in the pot. I wanted it to look as if I had top pair with a weak kicker or second pair, like K-6 suited or A-8 or the like. In fact, I would have called $375 more with any pair or any reasonable hand, and I knew that Howard knew this was the case. I wanted Howard to raise it up with his hand, so that I could move all-in and win a big pot. My quick, nonchalant call had set a trap perfectly for Howard to fall into.

Howard now asked if he could raise—I continued to look disinterested in the transpiring events—and another player said, "Yes, you can raise, since the raise was over one-half the original bet." I was thinking, "Please raise it, please raise it." Howard now announced, "I raise," and he began fiddling with his chips. Now I began drooling: Howard would raise, and I would move in and bust him! After about 30 seconds, which is a long time in the poker world, Howard announced, "I'm all in for $7,300 more." I quickly counted my chips with the intent of calling his bet immediately, when I suddenly thought, "No need to rush her; let me study Howard for a moment."

Now, I knew that I couldn't fold the top two pair here, no way, but what if Howard had 3-3 in the hole or 8-8? Then I would have only a few outs; I would need a king if Howard had, say, 8-8 as his hole cards (I would be a huge underdog). The more I focused on Howard, the more I began to fear that he had exactly a set of threes. Intuitively, I read superstrength when I studied him! Logically, Howard doesn't usually play K-x hands, especially after I limp in, in the first position. Thus, I didn't think he had two pair like K-3. Then I remembered that Howard had thought about raising the pot before the flop, which made me think he did have 3-3, or 8-8, or even A-A.

So I started to talk, to send out the message that I did indeed have the top two pair (I couldn't flip my hand up like I could have in the good old days, or even tell him that that's what I had, or I could be penalized). How would Howard react to this news of my being strong? As I (legally) announced that I was super-strong, Howard said to me, "What, do you have, Ad-3d?" I didn't like this question at all, and responded, "That's what I thought you had." His look right then struck me. Now I became convinced that Howard didn't have the Ad-3d (the one hand that it was easiest to assign to him here), and that one statement by him convinced me that I needed to fold my top two pair. You see, I knew Howard was super-strong from my read, so by letting him know that I had a super-strong hand (through my talking) I was able to determine that he did indeed want to be called (he didn't show any fear). If Howard hadn't said anything to me, I probably would have had to call him with my top two pair. I had even mentioned to Howard earlier that I was reading everyone at the table well, except him. So now it was time to fold, but it took me a while to convince myself that this absurd laydown could actually be right. I can't be certain, but it's possible that I have never before folded the top two pair in my life with a nonsuited or nonstraightening flop.

Howard could still have had A-A, A-K, K-Q, or the Ad-3d (although I ruled this out when he began to talk), but I was reading that he was extremely strong. Finally—it took me more than five minutes (sorry, table!)—I threw the hand away face up, saying, "I fold."

Chris Bjorin, another player at the table, said out loud: "That is the worst laydown I have ever seen in my entire life." Whereupon Howard flipped up 3-3, and Chris did a double take! In fact, Chris later said it was one of the *best* laydowns he had even seen in his life. And it all happened because one professor did too much professing. Thus, when Joe suggests that a good no-tell strategy is to keep as quiet as possible at the table, he is giving you good advice.

Chapter 11

High- and Low-Confidence Displays
Part V: Tells of the Eyes

It has been said that our eyes are windows into our minds, so perhaps we should check the two portals for a glimpse of some worthwhile tells. Some people don't trust information gained from studying the visual area of the face because, as one songwriter astutely noted, "your lyin' eyes" are capable of deception. Yet, when it comes to revealing positive and negative emotions, the eyes can be a very accurate barometer of our feelings because we have very little control over them. So, let's examine some specific eye behaviors that can help us achieve reliable and truthful tells at the tables.

Eye Blocking: All the News Not Fit to See

Our eyes, more remarkable than any camera, have evolved as the primary means by which we receive information from the world

Fig.59. Eye blocking by closing
the eyelids keeps out bad
news.

Fig.60. Another form of eye-
blocking behavior: finger
block.

around us. They also serve as the primary site where we block
outside data from coming in. This censoring behavior is called
eye blocking and is a survival mechanism that evolved to protect
the brain from "seeing" undesirable images.

Eye blocking takes place so often and in such a variety of
ways that most people miss it completely or ignore its very significant meaning. We perform eye blocks by closing our eyes or
placing the thumb and index fingers of one hand over our eyes.
Some individuals will cup their hand completely over their eyes,
or even place articles against their face, to block out the un-
wanted information.

Think about a time when someone came in and told you
bad news. Perhaps you did not notice, but most likely as you
heard the information your eyelids closed for a few moments.

Fig.61. Another form of eye-
blocking behavior: hand
block.

Fig.62. Another form of eye-
blocking behavior: finger
shade.

This type of blocking behavior is very ancient in origin and hardwired in our brains; even babies innately block within the womb
when they hear loud sounds. Throughout our lives, we exercise
this eye-blocking response, which, in reality, neither blocks our
thoughts nor the things that we hear. And yet we still do it, if for
no other reason than perhaps to give the brain a temporary re-
spite or to communicate our deepest sentiments. For whatever the
reason, the brain still compels us to perform this behavior, either
to protect us or communicate our feelings (see figures 59–62).

I have personally used eye-blocking behavior as a "tell" in
my work with the FBI. In one murder case, we asked a suspect a
series of questions. Every question began the same way: "If you
had committed this crime, would you have used a . . ." A new
ending was added to each question by mentioning different

weapons that could be used to kill someone. So, for example, the first question was "If you had committed this crime, would you have used a machete?" This was followed by a second inquiry: "If you had committed this crime, would you have used a stick?" Other questions followed using other weapons: a bat, a knife, an ice pick, and a hammer. After each question, the suspect was allowed to give his answer. Details of the murder weapon used in the crime were never revealed to the public, so to an honest person, each weapon had the same value or "threat potential," but not to the guilty party. To the person who committed the crime, only one weapon would be seen as a threat— the one actually used in the commission of the crime. When the suspect heard the question that included the term "ice pick," his eyelids came down hard and stayed down for a few moments until the next question and weapon was presented. With that behavior, we knew that this individual was the perpetrator because, in fact, an ice pick *was* the murder weapon. His eye block gave him away; his later confession sealed his fate.

Another time that an eye-blocking tell helped solve a case was in Puerto Rico, where a hotel was set on fire as the result of a labor dispute. A security guard came under investigation immediately. One of the ways we determined that he had nothing to do with setting the fire was by asking him some very specific questions as to where he was before the fire, at the time of the fire, and during the fire, and whether he set the fire. His eyes only blocked in response to one inquiry: where he was prior to the start of the fire. That showed us there was something he didn't like about that question, something he perceived as a threat. So we questioned him further on this topic, and he eventually admitted to leaving his post to visit his girlfriend, who also worked at the hotel. Unfortunately, while he was gone, the arsonists entered the area he should have been guarding and started the fire.

You don't need to be an FBI agent or wear a badge to use eye-blocking tells at the poker table. You just need to be alert to the behavior once it occurs, as it is often a rapid response that might go unnoticed without careful observation.

Because eye-blocking behaviors are usually associated with seeing things we don't like, one can assume they are *low-confidence* tells at the table. As with most other tells, the eye-blocking response is most reliable and valuable when it happens in the proper context: immediately after a significant poker-related event occurs. Thus, eye blocking by an opponent right after he views his hole cards or community cards, or possibly a raise by another player, is valuable intel you'll want to consider in playing your hand.

Eye Time to Stack Could Mean Chip Attack

In a previous chapter, I described a relatively well-recognized tell: when a player looks at his hand and then quickly reaches for his chips, it is normally a high-confidence display indicating the player is pleased with his cards and will probably be betting the hand. There is a visual equivalent to this tell. When a player views her hand and then her eyes shift quickly to her chips, it is also normally a high-confidence display indicating that she is happy with her cards and plans to play the hand. The critical factor here is the *lag time* between when she sees her cards and checks her chip stack. The less time that elapses between when a person sees her cards and checks her chips, the stronger the indication that a true tell is being displayed. Also, if a person never (or rarely) looks at his chips unless he intends to bet, noting when he *does* look at them can provide significant information. To make this assessment meaningful, you will need to establish a baseline reading on your opponents so you will know which ones normally look at their chips and which ones don't.

Dilation Suggests Elation; Constriction Suggests Affliction

Here is a powerful, but simple truth: when we like something, our pupils dilate; when we don't, they constrict. We have no conscious control over our pupils, which respond to both external stimuli (e.g., changes in light) and internal stimuli (e.g., thoughts) in a fraction of a second, a response that can easily be missed. These eye behaviors are very useful, but most people don't look for them, ignore them, or, when they see them, undervalue their utility. It doesn't help matters that the pupils are very small and that dark-colored eyes are more difficult to read than light-colored eyes.

What about pupillary changes at the poker table? If you can see them, they will provide accurate, valuable information about your opponents that is definitely worth obtaining. Basically, as people read their cards, you'll want to be reading their eyes. If they like what they see, their pupils will dilate (the iris of the eye will get smaller). If they are dissatisfied with the cards they are dealt, the pupils will constrict (see figures 63 and 64). It is easier to see pupil changes in people with blue and green eyes. Of course, players who wear sunglasses make pupil observation impossible, which is one of the reasons such eyewear is becoming increasingly popular at the tables.

If your vision is sharp enough and you can actually see pupil dilation and constriction in nearby opponents, don't

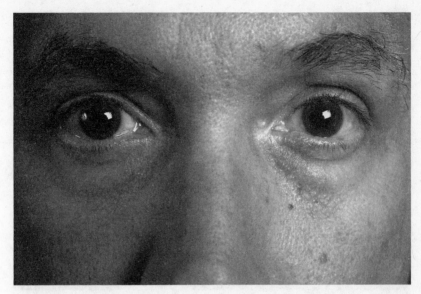

Fig.63. Papillary constriction indicative of stress or dislike.

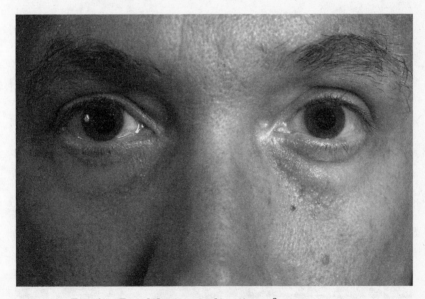

**Fig.64. Eye dilation indicative of contentment
and positive emotions.**

Fig. 65. Note normal eye appearance of player
when you first sit at the table.

Fig. 66. Squinting eyes reveal high discomfort, usually
because of a marginal situation.

forget to establish a pupillary baseline for each of them. What you are looking for are deviations from normal pupil size in response to specific poker-related events. Don't forget that pupil dilation and constriction can be caused by factors unrelated to poker—variation in lighting, medical conditions, drugs— and these changes can mislead you if you're not aware of why they are caused.

Beyond Pupillary Tells: Squinting Tries and Flashbulb Eyes

When the pupils don't constrict enough on their own, people will actually squint (subconsciously) as they see something or someone they don't like. While walking with my daughter recently, we passed someone she recognized. She squinted slightly as she gave the girl a low wave with her hand. I asked her who that was, suspecting something negative had transpired between them. She replied that the girl had been a high school classmate with whom she had previously had words. The low hand wave was social; the eye squint, an honest and betraying display of negative emotions and dislike (seven years in the making). She was unaware that her squinting behavior had given away her true feelings about the girl. Yet the information stood out like a beacon to me.

The same is true at the poker table. When players squint after looking at their cards, it is usually a low-confidence tell indicating dissatisfaction with what they have seen. They might be totally unaware they have transmitted this information, but for those players who watch for such nonverbal behaviors, the tell is unmistakable (see figures 65 and 66).

Some players—besides squinting—will lower their eyebrows

Fig. 67. Lowered eyebrows appear when players
are less confident.

**Fig. 68. Arching eyebrows are a good indication
of positive feelings.**

after observing something significant at the table. Whereas arched eyebrows are a sign of high confidence, lowered eyebrows are a sign of low confidence, a behavior that indicates weakness and insecurity in the player (see figures 67 and 68). Prisoners have reported in studies that when new inmates arrive, they look for this lowered-eyebrow behavior, which lets them know who among the newcomers are weak and insecure. It is also a tell *you* can capitalize on in probing for weakness and strength in your opponents, both in their play and in the cards they hold.

What about pupil dilation? Well, as is the case with constriction, people will sometimes add to the effect by further modifying their eye behavior. For example, when people see something or someone they like, not only will their pupils enlarge, so will their eyes! When we see something positive, we tend to raise our eyebrows (eyebrow arching) to make them as big as possible, consistent with the pupillary dilation. In addition, some people also arch their eye orbits, which expands the eyes even farther, and leads to an appearance known as *flashbulb eyes*. Raising of the eyebrows works in conjunction with expansion of the eye orbits to create that wide-eyed look normally associated with positive events.

When playing poker, a good "eyedicator" of high confidence and a strong hand is a person who, upon seeing her cards, gets that wide-eyed look—eye orbits expanded, eyebrows arched. Experienced players and professionals try to avoid such dramatic tells, but, even for them, it is not an easy task to accomplish. In the moment of elation that comes with seeing good things like pocket aces or a nut flush on the flop, people often forget to control their emotions, and those flashbulb eyes light up the room. This should help illuminate your most effective strategy as you play out the hand.

Phil's Student Becomes a Good Pupil and Reveals the Importance of Eye Tells

If you're an "I'm from Missouri" kind of person who says "show me" before you believe something, then you're going to enjoy this story about the power of tells in playing effective poker. It all happened during a freeze-out tournament at my first Camp Hellmuth. I was at a table with ESPN Poker Club columnist and producer Andrew Feldman when the following hand unfolded: Andrew bet out with a pocket pair of sevens and I called with pocket nines. The flop came 8, 6, 4 rainbow. Andrew raised and I just called, planning to trap him. The turn card was an eight that paired the board. Andrew made another bet and I called, sensing some weakness in my opponent. The river was a seven, and now Andrew made a large bet. Remembering that Joe had just discussed how a player's eyes dilate when he sees something he likes, I stared directly into Andrew's eyes right after the seven hit the board. I couldn't believe it! His eyes dilated as I studied his face. Right then and there, I suspected I had lost the hand but won an excellent opportunity to illustrate the power of what the students were learning. I picked up the microphone and announced to the seminar participants that because I had detected one of Joe's tells in my opponent, I was going to lay down my pocket nines because the dilation in Andrew's eyes convinced me that the seven had made his hand unbeatable. Sure enough, Andrew flipped over his pocket sevens to reveal a full house: sevens over eights.

Writing about the experience in his poker column, this is the way Andrew described the experience and his accompanying emotions:

"Thanks, Joe," Phil Hellmuth says as he folds his hand.

I [Andrew Feldman] sat in Seat 2 of the feature table, dazed and wondering what I gave away. I didn't move. I didn't think I acted too quickly or that my bet on the river was inadequate. I didn't blink an eye.

Hellmuth grabs the microphone and begins his explanation to the entire tournament field before I can rake in the chips.

"Joe, you said this morning, when someone's eyes dilate, they see something they like," Hellmuth said. "When that seven hit the river, his eyes dilated. Thanks, Joe."

Oh man.

What the heck was that, Andrew?!? Go get some sunglasses!

I couldn't believe it. I stood up and yelled out, "Thanks, Joe," receiving modest laughter.

Yeah, thanks a lot, Mr. FBI. You cost me another $900 in chips.

Hellmuth had a perfect read on me. The seven on the river, which incidentally was a huge suckout, gave me a full house, sevens over eights.

Although each of the seminars was interesting and informative, none compared with Navarro's lecture on reading people. One word: amazing. Even Hellmuth and Cloutier took notes during it.

I wish they hadn't.*

---

* Andrew Feldman's article appeared on August 24, 2005. It can be found at http://proxy.espn.go.com/espn/poker/columns/story?columnist=feldman_andrew&id=2141913.

Chapter 12

Pacifying Behaviors and Poker Tells

I am going to make you an offer you can't refuse: I'm going to give you $1 million if you can prove to me that you've never experienced *stress* in your life.

How can I afford to make this offer? Because I know with certainty that no one will ever collect the money. Stress is a condition we all experience. It can be caused by many things: for example, frustrations, time binds, overwork, emotional conflicts, or the loss of a loved one. We live in stressful times surrounded by stressful circumstances. The only way to eliminate stress in our lives is to eliminate life itself, for it is only in death that we are truly free of stress.

In the course of human development, we, as a species, have developed a repertoire of *pacifying behaviors* to help our bodies deal with stress. These are behaviors that the brain needs and which it has adapted to comfort itself when faced with internal and/or external stressors. We see this kind of behavior in infants and young children when they suck their thumb or a (appropriately named) pacifier. As we grow older, we develop other pacifiers to relieve stress. It is almost as if the brain is saying, "Hey, body, do something to calm me down . . . pacify me." And when we comply, the brain rewards those pacifying behaviors that have the desired effect, and we tend to repeat them again in future stressful situations.

"Houston, We Have a Problem . . ."

If you want to see the dramatic relationship between stress and pacifying behavior, you need look no further than the Mission Control Center in Houston on that fateful day in 1970 when the Apollo 13 astronauts announced, "Houston, we have a problem." If you study the videos of the Mission Control Center personnel, you will see that almost everyone was engaged in some sort of pacifying behavior. These workers were suddenly confronted with a high-stress situation and their brains were saying, "Do something about it; calm me down." And they did. We know that any hand-to-body touching can be calming, particularly in sensitive areas like the face and neck . . . and that is what the engineers, scientists, and technicians were doing in Mission Control: they were massaging their necks, stroking their faces, rubbing their foreheads, licking their lips. These pacifying behaviors didn't help the Mission Control personnel solve the Apollo 13 problem; rather, it helped keep them calm as they worked to that end.

When people are under high stress, there is a definite increase in pacifying behaviors. Some of these behaviors will also become more pronounced, as in the case of one Mission Control supervisor who began chewing his gum more vigorously when the problem was discovered, or a college student who smoked more cigarettes on class days when there were tests rather than the standard lectures.

Which brings us to the topic of poker. Poker is classified as a game. Games are normally thought of as entertainment, pleasant diversions from the rigors of life in which the participants have fun engaging in some playful activity. When poker is played this way, at home, for toothpicks or maybe with nickel-dime-quarter limits, you aren't going to see much stress or, predictably, much pacifying behavior, either. There's no need for it. However, when we start "playing" poker for meaningful money—particularly the multimillion-dollar pots contested in WPT and WSOP tournaments—then there will be plenty of stress and the pacifying behaviors that accompany it.

So how can you, the reader, benefit from all this? As you play for increasingly higher stakes, stress will become an increasingly significant factor at the table, and it is then that your knowledge of pacifying tells will aid you in reading on your opponent(s). Here are some guidelines to help you understand and utilize pacifying behavioral tells most effectively in poker.

1. *You need to recognize pacifying behaviors when they occur.* I will identify the most common ones for you in a few moments.

2. *You need to establish a pacifying baseline for each opponent* when things are calm at the table (usually when a player is between hands or already out of a hand). Some players will self-pacify throughout their time at the table; others won't pacify at all except when their stress levels rise significantly. By identifying a player's

baseline behavior, you can note any increase and/or intensity in pacifying behaviors and react accordingly.

3. *When you see an opponent make a pacifying gesture, you need to stop and ask yourself, "What caused him to do that?"* You know that the player feels uneasy about something; your job is to find out what that something is.

4. *Pacifying behaviors almost always are used to calm a person after a stressful event occurs;* thus, as a general principle, you can assume that if a player is engaged in pacifying behavior, some stressful event has preceded it and caused it to happen.

5. *Stress behaviors are most likely to occur immediately after significant actions at the poker table,* primarily when players see new card(s) or bets (particularly large raises or reraises). Thus, this is the time to watch for them and any pacifying behaviors that follow.

6. *The ability to link a pacifying behavior with the specific stressor that caused it can help you play your opponent more effectively.* If, for example, Player A puts in a big raise and, upon seeing this, Player B immediately begins to rub the back of his neck (a pacifying behavior), that bet has caused enough stress that Player B's brain is begging to be pacified. This should serve as a clue that the bet has upset Player B, and you'll want to consider that information in your play of the hand. What does Player B's behavior suggest? Possibly that he doesn't want to risk that much money, and so the size of the bet stressed him and now he is pacifying to calm down. A more likely inference is that Player B doesn't have the hand strength to call or come over the

top of Player A's raise, and *that* is what has created the stress and resultant pacifying behavior.

7. *Pacifying behaviors can help you read a person more effectively when they are accompanied by other tells.* Thus, you should be attempting to spot multiple tells whenever possible to make better overall judgments about a person's intentions and hand strength. For example, if you see a player press her lips together after seeing the flop (low-confidence tell) and then put in a big bet, followed by a pacifying behavior (stroking the face or licking the lips), you can be more certain she has a weak hand and is pacifying to relieve the stress of bluffing. Another example: if the turn card is revealed and you see a player lean away from the table (low-confidence tell) and then pacify (rub his forehead), you can be relatively certain the card didn't help his hand!

8. *Note what part of the body a person pacifies.* This is significant, because the higher the stress, the greater the amount of facial or neck stroking is involved.

9. *Observe the intensity (frequency, pressure applied) of the pacifying behavior.* If a person is a smoker and he is stressed, he will smoke more. If he chews gum, he will chew faster.

10. *Although not always true, one should always consider that a player is bluffing if he shows pacifying behaviors immediately after making a big bet at the pot.* One tournament player who is often on television has a habit of puffing out his cheeks and then slowly exhaling through his lips. This is a pacifying behavior, and he consistently does this when he's on a bluff.

11. *Recall that the higher the stakes, the greater the stress;*
     and the greater the stress, the more pacifying behav-
     iors you will see at the table.

Pacifying Behavioral Tells to Watch for at the Poker Tables

Over the course of human evolution, certain "standard" pacifying behaviors have emerged to help calm us down in the aftermath of stressful situations. I'm going to describe them for you now. When you see them during a game, take advantage of your observation—using the 11 guidelines just presented—to better read your opponent and enhance your chances of winning at the table.

Pacifying Behaviors Involving the Neck

Neck touching and/or stroking is one of the most significant and frequent pacifying behaviors we use in responding to stress. Some people rub the back of their neck with their fingers; others stroke the sides of their neck or just under the chin above the Adam's apple, tugging at the fleshy area of the neck. This area is rich with nerve endings that, when stroked, reduce blood pressure, lower the heart rate, and calm the individual down. It is here, also, where the vagus nerve traverses down the neck. As one Camp Hellmuth attendee emphasized, "What happens in vagus, stays calm in Vegas." Yes, he was allowed to graduate.

I have observed over the decades that there are gender differences in the way men and women use the neck to pacify themselves (see figures 69–74). Men usually are more robust in their movements, grasping or cupping the front of their neck (under the chin) with their hand and stimulating their vagus nerve as a means of pacification. Sometimes they will stroke the sides or the back of the neck with their fingers, or adjust their tie knot or shirt collar. Women do things differently. When they pacify using the neck, they will sometimes touch, twist, or otherwise manipulate necklaces they are wearing. The other major way women neck-pacify is by covering their *suprasternal notch* with their hand. The supra (which comes from terms meaning "above" and "breastbone") notch is the hollow area right below the Adam's apple that is sometimes referred to as the *neck dimple*. Women touch their hand to this part of their neck and/or cover it when they feel stressed; for example, when they feel threatened, fearful, uncomfortable . . . or anxious at the poker table.

This covering of the suprasternal notch is a relatively significant tell. It can be used to detect when a person is bluffing, both in life and in poker. I remember one FBI investigation in which we thought an armed and dangerous fugitive might be hiding out at his mother's home. Another agent and I went to the woman's house, and when we knocked at the door, she came outside to meet us. We showed our identification and began asking her a series of questions. When I inquired, "Is your son in the house?" she put her hand to her suprasternal notch and said, "No, he's not." I noted her behavior, and we continued with our questioning. After a few minutes I asked, "Is it possible that while you were at work, your son could have sneaked into the house?" Once again, she put her hand up to her neck dimple and replied, "No, I'd know that." I was now confident that her son was in the house, because the only time she moved her hand to her neck was when I suggested that possibility. To make absolutely sure my assumption was correct, we continued to speak with the woman until, as we prepared to leave, I made one last

Fig.69. Touching the neck in
the front is an indicator of
discomfort or distress.

Fig.70. Touching the neck on
the side is also a pacifier.

inquiry: "Just so I can finalize my records, you're *positive* he's
not in the house, right?" For a third time, her hand went to her
neck as she affirmed her earlier answer. I was now certain the
woman was lying. A search of the house turned up her missing
son hiding in a bedroom closet.

Men perform a variant of this behavior, but it is more subtle. Men will play with their tie knot or bring their shirt collar
together as if to cover up their neck. Regardless, it is still an indicator of distress that occurs in real time and should be capital-
ized upon by the savvy poker player who realizes this is a sign of
weakness.

There's an interesting footnote to this incident. When I was
involved in the Discovery Channel show with Annie Duke, I noticed that when something disturbed her, she pacified by covering

Fig.71. Massaging the back of the neck is definitely indicative of distress.

Fig.72. Women cover their neck dimple when they are stressed or fearful.

her suprasternal notch. I said to her, "You really need to watch that neck-touching response, because if I can see it, so can your opponents at the poker table. I suspect you might display that behavior when you're bluffing, and other players might decipher it and realize you have a weak hand." After I identified the behavior, she actually recognized she had been touching her neck in such a manner and said she would make an effort to stop. To her credit, I haven't seen her doing it at the tables since our discussion.

Pacifying Behaviors Involving the Face

Touching or stroking the face is a frequent human pacifying response to stress. Stroking the face, rubbing the forehead, touching, rubbing, or licking the lip(s), pulling or massaging the

**Fig.73. Playing with neck   Fig.74. Men adjust tie knots
jewelry is a modification of   when stressed or
neck-dimple touching.   concerned.**

earlobe with thumb and forefinger, stroking the nose or beard, playing with the hair—all of these behaviors can serve to pacify an individual in the face of a stressful situation. Some people pacify by puffing out their cheeks and then slowly exhaling (see figures 75–79).

Pacifying Behaviors Involving Sounds

Whistling can be a pacifying behavior (see figure 80). Some people whistle to calm themselves when they are walking in a strange area of a city or down a dark, deserted corridor or road. I was at a table where a player all of a sudden caught himself whistling right after he had bluffed. He whistled to pacify himself, because

Fig.75. Exhaling through puffed cheeks is a very good indicator of distress.

Fig.76. Face stroking can help to calm nerves when stressed or bluffing.

he was afraid he would be caught bluffing and lose. He did. Some people even talk to pacify themselves in times of stress. This can be significant if a person who has been quiet throughout a poker session suddenly turns chatty. If this happens, you should ask yourself, "Why is this person suddenly talking? Is it because his brain is saying, 'Calm me down!'" If it happens right after the person puts in a big raise, you might consider the possibility of a bluff. If it occurs after an individual sees his cards but *before* he has to call or raise some other player's bet, you might suspect that the player is stressed by needing to decide whether he wants to get involved in the pot with the cards he has. This would suggest that he has a weak or borderline hand.

Fig.77. Forehead rubbing can   **Fig.78. Earlobe pulling is**
help to calm nerves.   **used to pacify.**

The Leg Cleanser

One pacifying behavior that is not always easy to see (because it takes place under the table) is the leg cleanser. This is where a person takes his hand and rubs it over his pants leg (pants brushing), as if he were cleaning it, or wiping it off. Some individuals will do it only one time, but often it is done over and over. This tell is a good indication that someone is under stress and, therefore, is worth looking for. One way to try to spot the behavior is to watch any opponent who puts his arm under the table. If he is doing a leg cleanser, you will normally see his upper arm and shoulder moving in harmony with the hand as it rubs along the side of the leg (see figures 81 and 82).

Fig.79. Women will play with their hair to soothe themselves.

Fig. 80. Whistling can help to calm nerves when bluffing.

Fig.81. Hands on legs are used to rub sweat away and to pacify the player.

Fig.82. Leg rub calms players down, especially when they have a rag hand.

The Ventilator

This behavior involves a person (usually a male) putting his fingers between his shirt collar and neck and pulling the fabric away from his skin. This "ventilating" action is often a reaction to stress, and is a good indicator that the person is unhappy with his hand and/or other significant events occurring at the table (see figure 83).

The Self-Administered Body Hug

This is the pacifying behavior made famous by Phil. When facing stressful circumstances, some individuals will pacify by crossing their arms and rubbing their hands against their shoulders (see

Fig. 83. Neck ventilation is a very accurate indicator of distress.

Fig. 84. Hugging oneself is very indicative
of distress or concern.

figure 84). Watching a person employ this pacifying behavior is remindful of the way a mother hugs a young child. It is a protective posture. On the other hand, if you see a person with his arms crossed in front of him, leaning forward and giving you a defiant look, this is *not* a pacifying behavior!

In a sense, pacifying behaviors are "supporting players" in our plot to read people successfully as we pursue a happy ending to our poker play. Taken alone, they can be helpful, but their usefulness is greatest when combined with the "major players" (the tells described in earlier chapters). It is in these circumstances that pacifying behaviors can help us make finer discriminations in judgment and more certain determinations in how to handle our opponents at the table.

Chapter 13

"Going Hollywood" in the
Age of Perception Management

They lurk at the casino poker tables, waiting for their cue. If you've put in reasonable hours at the game, you've seen them make their entrance. I'm speaking, of course, of that individual dubbed the "Poker Thespian." This character has taken Shakespeare literally, and believes that when the bard says, "All the world's a stage," it includes the poker table where you just happen to be sitting. It is here where he puts on an act—known as "going Hollywood"—to achieve one or both of the following objectives.

1. He displays an aggressive persona to intimidate you and either (a) make you fold your hand or (b) become so unnerved that you play less effectively. He does this by aggressive staring, territorial invasion of your space, and/or inflammatory verbal comments disparaging your poker skills.

2. He showboats (exhibits loud, obnoxious, aggressive,

insulting, boorish behavior) to encourage media attention, better name recognition, and, hopefully, lucrative
endorsement deals. This behavior is of relatively recent
origin, growing out of televised poker matches where
a tantrum-throwing, in-your-face player can increase
Nielson ratings and his own celebrity standing at the
same time. Unfortunately, you can sometimes get caught
in the line of fire in his attempt to play to the cameras.

It is in your best interest to ignore players who are going
Hollywood. Otherwise, paraphrasing what Clint Eastwood used
to say, you're going to make their day. As I emphasized in chapter 2, getting caught up in testosterone-driven combat will only
detract from your ability to play solid, reasoned poker.

Although there is nothing illegal about going Hollywood
and/or showboating, I believe both demonstrate disrespect for
the game, and I, for one, wouldn't recommend engaging in either
behavior. On the other hand, acting—without the coarse tinge of
Hollywood showboaters—is a deeply ingrained and legitimate
aspect of poker used by players to outmaneuver their opponents
and win more money at the tables. In the FBI, we refer to this
type of stagecraft as perception management.

Perception Management

Perception management is the process by which an individual
creates an image of himself that, if believed by others, will benefit him. The image does not have to be true; in fact, many times
(particularly in undercover FBI work) perception management
involves creating an image of yourself that is totally at odds with

reality (think of an undercover drug agent). In effect, the FBI agent, through perception management, is bluffing. He is pretending to be something he is not . . . and hoping he can get away with it so he can gain the confidence and, eventually, the arrest and conviction of the bad guys.

At the poker table, we use perception management to fool our opponents into believing something that isn't true. When you're nervous, you appear to be cool, calm, and collected. When you're struggling with something, it's like you're not bothered by it. *You want to make your opponents believe as you want them to believe, and you do this by behaving in a manner that will convince them to act in accordance with your wishes.*

Consider perception management when it comes to bluffing. Many players—even amateurs—will attempt to convince you that they are strong when they're weak, and weak when they're strong. For instance, a player might bluff by scowling and looking discouraged when she's got monster cards and display a confident smile when she's got nothing in her hand but dreams.

To the person trained in observing tells, watching an opponent who is inexperienced in faking is no contest, really. The fake tells are readily recognized by their *exaggerated, unnatural* quality. The behavior is so stilted that it looks contrived; it doesn't flow naturally, and the "actor" holds the "pose" (tell) too long. In addition, the behavior is transparent because it appears over the top, too outrageous and cocky to be taken seriously. The would-be bluffer tends to adopt actions that are at opposite ends of the behavioral continuum: either he is suddenly friendly toward an opponent or aggressively staring her down, acting nonchalant or talking excessively and showing unusual levels of enthusiasm. In fact, many individuals who fake tells of confidence exhibit *exuberance* over *investment;* in other words, their nonverbal enthusiasm exceeds their willingness to invest. "I got a great hand," they claim, but then they don't make a bet to match their words. They don't put their money where their mouth is, and when exuberance outstrips *pot investment* it should make you stop and ask why. These same individuals have a tendency to convince (overstated emphasis) rather than convey (simple, non-repetitive) information: they make multiple efforts at trying to persuade you they have a very good or bad hand. In all of these cases, to the trained observer, the Poker Thespian's bad acting is more of a giveaway than no acting at all.

But what about the person who practices and polishes his tells so that he can use them against you in a kind of reverse psychology? There is always the chance of this happening, but it isn't as easy as it sounds and, furthermore, there are ways to detect these false tells. Consider these points:

1. It takes talent to execute a false tell effectively. This is because the person bent on deception must fight his ingrained tendency to go with his natural limbic response when portraying the opposite emotion.

2. A skilled observer will be watching for multiple tells—or tell clusters—revealed by an opponent. A player who is trying to fake a tell often gives herself away by a second, contradictory nonverbal behavior. This is why I emphasize that congruent, supporting tells make for more assurance of accuracy. Contradictory tells should put a person on alert for possible deception. For example, before I'd believe the player who showed facial disgust with her cards (bluffing weakness), I'd want to couple that behavior with some other supporting tells. If I couldn't find any, I'd be very cautious. I'd also be

interested in the position of her feet. If I see that her feet are in the ready position but her upper body is pretending not to be, I'll always go with the most honest part of the body, which is the feet, and assume she is going to take action, rather than fold her hand.

3. False tells often seem stilted or unnatural.

4. You can't use tells to deceive someone if you don't know about him in the first place. People who haven't read this book (and there will be many of them) will be unaware of the tells discussed in these pages and, thus, unable to utilize them for deceptive purposes. Meanwhile, they remain vulnerable by unknowingly giving off their own tells that readers of this volume can recognize and use to their advantage.

5. By observing specific players over time, you will learn which ones are giving off false tells and which ones are exhibiting real ones. The better you know your opponent, the easier it will be to make this determination. There is always the danger that once someone knows about a tell, they can try to use it to deceive; but, in general, the more tells you can identify and the better your observational skills, the more often you will benefit from knowing someone's tells than be fooled by them.

When a Feign Becomes a Pain

One tell that needs to be interpreted and/or used with extreme caution involves *feigning disinterest* during a poker game (see figure 85). Consider, as an example, this scenario: In the middle of a hand, a person looks away from the table, feigning disinter-

Fig.85. Feigning disinterest by looking away is a poor bluff often seen at poker tables.

est. What does this mean? This tell has been out there for so long that it turns out players use it for diametrically opposed reasons: (1) to make an opponent think they're not interested in the hand when they really are (bluffing weakness when they are strong); (2) to make an opponent think their cards are so good that they don't even worry about losing the pot (bluffing strength when they are weak). Therefore, I'd not place much value in this non-verbal behavior. It's not a clear-cut tell. At a minimum, I'd want to see if there were any low- or high-confidence cues associated with the feigning of disinterest behavior, as well as any signs of engagement or pacifying activities.

Is a Person Who Practices "Concealing, Not Revealing" Using Perception Management?

Not really. Individuals who are attempting to conceal their tells are in a passive mode. They are trying to avoid giving information away. Individuals who use perception management are in the active mode; they are purposely trying to give information away, but in a manner to manipulate the thinking of their opponents. The "conceal, don't reveal" player is trying to hide and/or eliminate tells; the perception management player is trying to reveal and transmit tells to gain a tactical advantage at the tables.

The Reality of Perception Management

Today, there are so few people who make a concentrated effort to read tells in others that I wouldn't worry too much about individuals purposely using tells to fake you out at the tables. It's something to be aware of, naturally, but not something to obsess about.

It is generally understood that players go through three stages of development as they mature in their poker skills. In the first stage, they *play their cards*. There is little or no concern for what else is taking place at the table. In the second stage, the focus expands to include *what cards the opponents hold*. It is during this stage that the player becomes aware of—and utilizes—tells to try to gain insight into the strength of an opponent's hand. In the third stage, the player takes a final step and considers *what cards his opponents think* he *has*. It is in this final stage that perception management becomes an issue, as the player takes steps to disguise and/or fool opponents about the strength of his or her hand.

If you are already well versed in nonverbal behavior and can read people successfully (stage two), then you might attempt a bit of perception management (stage three) by using tells for deceptive purposes against your opponents. However, before you can get players to believe you have a super-hand (when you don't), you'll need to literally rewire your nervous system to override normal limbic responses so that you can adapt all of the subtle behaviors that are equated with confidence: erect posture, torso shift toward the table, dilation of the nose, breathing deeply rather than holding the breath, thumbs in a high position, and arms appropriately positioned on the table. If you can do all this in a way that others think are genuine, and they're savvy enough to even *look* for these behaviors, then you might be able to move to an even higher level in your climb to poker stardom.

Frankly, I'll be more than satisfied if you're able to successfully (a) conceal, not reveal, your own tells; and (b) detect tells in your opponents and use that information to increase your winning percentage at the tables. If you can achieve these two goals, you will be a formidable poker player against any opponent whenever and wherever the game is played.

How I Used Perception Management Against the Master

Joe tells us that perception management is the process by which an individual creates an image of himself that, if believed by others, will benefit him. I try to do this through what I call a "false tell": a manufactured motion, movement, or speech pattern, or simply the way you push your chips into the pot, that sends a subtle signal to your opponents that you are strong when you are weak, or weak when you are strong. The most opportune time to use a false tell would be during a key pot: a pot worth winning, a pot that you really want to manipulate others into. If you overuse the false tell, it will lead people to see your "tells" in a different light, thus rendering the tactic ineffective in the future.

One time I used a false tell was at the Taj Mahal Casino's $7,000 buy-in No-Limit Hold'em Championship event in Atlantic City in October 2000. During the tournament the following hand developed: with the blinds at $100–$200, three players called the original bet, and from the small blind I opted to call as well, with 4-4. With a flop of Qh-4s-2d, I checked with my nearly unbeatable hand. From there, it went check (big blind), check, check, and then Men "the Master" Nguyen bet out $600. Now I quickly decided to use my best false tell as I raised it up $1,200 more to go. I wanted to use my false tell in order to lure Men—or the other players in the pot—into paying me the most chips possible. About an hour earlier I had made a nice-sized bluff, and after I was called, I committed to memory all of the motions and looks that I had made during the bluff. Now, versus Men, I put my chips into the pot the same way, I talked in the same manner, I leaned back in my chair to the same extent, and finally I looked right at Men, just as I had earlier, when my bluff had been exposed.

Men took the bait and called my $1,200 raise. The next card was the 6s, for a board of Qh-4s-2D-6s, and I decided to bet the same percentage of the pot that I had bet during my last bluff. I bet out $2,500 again, with all of the same mannerisms I had affected during my real bluff. Men called the $2,500 and I decided I would bet $4,000 on the end if a seemingly safe card came up.

The 9h that came up on the river looked to me like the safest card in the world, and I followed through with my plan of betting $4,000, with all of my false-tell mannerisms intact. I was now praying for a call from Men, when I realized he was thinking of raising me! Finally, he merely called my $4,000 bet, and I confidently flipped up my trip fours (three of a kind) and waited for the pot to be pushed to me. After a few seconds Men flipped up his hand, pocket nines—which he had tripped up on the last card—to take the pot from me.

Although I lost this pot, on the last card, I had controlled Men's play through a series of well-executed false tells.

Joe is correct when he says if you're able to successfully conceal, not reveal, your own tells, and at the same time detect tells in your opponents and use that information effectively, you will be a formidable poker player. What I'm suggesting is when you reach that skill level you might want to add the false tell to your playing repertoire and give yourself one more weapon in your winning arsenal.

Chapter 14

What You Should Know to Vanquish a Pro

I'm going to describe a hypothetical event. If it happened to you, I want you to decide if it would be a dream fulfilled or a nightmare come true. You've just arrived in Las Vegas where the World Series of Poker is contested once a year. You decide to try your luck at a super satellite tournament to see if you can win your way into the "Big One" (the $10,000 World Championship). What the heck, it only costs $250 bucks to take a shot. So you plunk down your money, get your randomized seating assignment, and go to your table. There, sitting across from you, is a bona fide poker legend, someone like Phil Hellmuth, Phil Ivey, Lyle Berman, Annie Duke, or Johnny Chan. This is your first chance to play against a true poker champion; your first opportunity to test your skills and cunning against the best in the business.

So, what's your decision? Is this "opportunity" something you've always dreamed about or a nightmare that's kept you awake at night? If you answered, "A dream fulfilled," then I applaud your courage and faith in what you've just learned!

If you answered, "A nightmare come true," I can understand your sentiment—I don't know if I'd want to play in a foursome with Tiger Woods, either—but I think I can ease your fears and show you that playing against pros is not as forbidding as it may seem. In fact, as an unknown, you might present more of a threat to them than vice versa.

What Are My Chances of Playing Against a Pro, Anyway?

Surprisingly better than you might think. The reason I am including this section in the book is because I believe many of you will participate in online and land-based tournaments where pros also play. These don't have to be the $10,000 to $25,000 championships, either. Many pros play in the lower-cost satellites and tournaments, and in reasonably priced no-limit ring (cash) games. (In the Caesars Palace Poker Room, Cyndy Violette was sitting two seats over from the author playing no-limit Hold 'em with $10 and $20 blinds.)

If you should find yourself in competition against a famous pro player, you need to adopt the right mental attitude, and then you need to play poker as usual. Well, almost as usual . . . I truly believe that playing against a pro will help you elevate your game (who doesn't want to play their best against the best), which, in the final analysis, is another reason why playing against professionals shouldn't scare you; it should be viewed as an opportunity for learning and earning.

Don't Let the Professional Mystique Cause a Psychological Mistake

The first thing you need to do when you recognize (or discover) a poker champion at your table is realize you're going to be in awe of this player. It's a natural reaction, nothing to be ashamed of. Don't be afraid to exhibit a bit of hero worship and even deferential behavior to this living legend when you first meet him or her.

The second thing you need to do is *get over it!* Once the cards are in the air and the game has begun, you have to get the stars out of your eyes and onto your cards. Remember, poker is the only big money sport I know of where a rank amateur can play against a ranked professional and stand a chance of winning. It happens *all* the time. Why? Because in the short run (an afternoon of play, or even a five-day tournament), luck can have its moments, and if your cards are right, on a lucky day, you can beat anyone. It is true that if you sat down and played head-to-head with a guy like Phil Hellmuth for eight hours a day over the span of a year, you'd be a loser. Luck would even out and skill would prevail. But, again, in a tournament or a ring game that lasts a matter of hours or days, we're not speaking of long term, we're speaking of short term, and in the short term *anything* can happen, and "anything" includes the opportunity for you to come away with the money and the glory. Sadly, even in the short run, this *won't* happen if your mind can't accept the fact that it is possible. If you let your awe of a professional opponent wreck havoc with your own game, you're going to lose. Why? Because you're a 2-to-1 underdog, battling your opponent *and* yourself!

The "Bowling Score Effect"

In the late 1960s, behavioral scientists conducted a study in which they observed how bowlers would perform when paired with other keglers of equal and higher status. They discovered what came to be known as the "bowling score effect:" in the presence of a higher-status individual, a good bowler would actually score lower than normal in a show of striking (or should I say nonstriking) deference to the higher-status individual. This bowling score effect has been replicated in other sporting events and in human behavior in general. If you think of the way we treat our heroes in the United States and the deference we afford them, I think you'll see what I'm talking about. (Some would say we show such deference that high-status individuals can get away with murder! I'll leave that for you to decide.)

The point here is that you must overcome your natural tendency to be deferential to a poker player you perceive to be superior to yourself. Yes, it is daunting to play the big-name stars; even they admit to being intimidated the first time *they* were in a similar position. Nobody starts at the top of the poker mountain; every player will have to endure the challenge of facing better-known opponents as they climb (claw?) his or her way to the pinnacle of poker performers.

In summary, then, when you face a poker legend at your table (particularly if it's the first time), take these steps.

1.   Allow yourself a moment to be awed by your opponent and savor the idea of playing against a living legend.
2.   Once play begins, *don't* let this sense of awe continue. Overcome your tendency to be intimidated by your

well-known opponent and don't fall victim to the bowling score effect.

3. Understand that you have a reasonable chance of beating even the most accomplished professional when the playing time is short, which gives luck a larger role in determining the outcome of the competition. These are the playing conditions you will be experiencing, and they are in your favor.

4. Use the knowledge that you are playing against a top-flight professional to motivate you; to encourage you to bring your A game to the table. Even if you lose, think how much better you'll feel if you believe you earned that professional's respect because of the way you played.

5. Remember that no matter *who* is sitting at the table, the chips haven't changed in value, the cards are the same, the statistics still hold, luck still plays a role, and anyone can win. Concentrate on what you know and play your game. There are eight other people you have to worry about; the pro is just one of them.

6. Recognize that you actually have certain advantages when playing against top-flight competition that can actually *increase* your chances of winning. I'll discuss these advantages now.

Establish the Proper Frame of Mind for Beating the Pros at Their Own Game

I have heard several poker pros claim they would rather play against other pros than amateur or intermediate players. Why?

Because the pros are *predictable;* there is order and reason in their moves, calculation and knowledge in the decisions they make. If a pro skillfully represents a hand to another professional, there is an expectation that the move will work because the opposing player is sufficiently poker savvy to comprehend the move. Similarly, if a professional makes a big bet to thin the competition before the flop, she doesn't expect an opponent to see the bet (or even raise it!) with an 8-2 offsuit. One pro lamented, "What good does it do to bluff or skillfully bet or even change gears if you can't get a person off a hand?"

The problem is, when a professional player is confronted with an opponent of unknown talent and experience, that opponent is a kind of *wild card* that adds unpredictability and chaos to the game. That means, in a kind of perverse sense, that the professional *fears* the newcomer because he has no read on either the person's card sense or his ability to detect tells. Given the time, the professional could probably determine a less-experienced player's strengths and weaknesses, strategies and tells. Note I say, "Given the time." But in the meantime—in the short period of time *you,* the unknown commodity—sit at the table, you present a dilemma and a threat to the pros. They don't know how you play, why you play the way you do, and how much skill is involved in your various moves. Particularly in no-limit Hold'em contests, where one bad move can cost *any* player his or her tournament life, you really have a stunning advantage over the pros because they don't know you and *you know them.*

This brings me to suggest that just as pros find you difficult because you are unpredictable, you should find them easier because they are more predictable. You can make moves on professionals because, properly executed, they will see and respond to them in the manner you intended. If you are fortunate, you might also know something of a specific professional's style of play. Maybe you read one of their books, or saw them on television or read about them in a magazine.

Doyle Brunson has regretted publishing his Super/System poker strategy because, once he did, everyone became aware of how he played and took advantage of that knowledge to cut into his profits and his success at the table. Many of the top players have been accurately categorized by their degree of aggressiveness and the playing strategies they employ. If you happen to be facing a professional whose play has been analyzed, and you are aware of this information, it gives you a significant edge during play. You know his or her playing style, and he or she knows nothing of yours. Which player would *you* rather be?

In establishing the proper psychological mind-set when playing professionals, keep these points in mind.

1. The professional has no idea of how you play and your level of sophistication. You represent randomness where the professional desires certainty; you are a *wild card* that can play effectively because your top-tier opponent will have difficulty putting you on a hand and be forced to play more defensively.

2. You will have a basic understanding of how the professional plays, because most championship-caliber players have certain standard rules of engagement and disengagement based on a working knowledge of the game's logic and mathematical probabilities. This will help you as you consider your playing options. In addition, you might have extra knowledge of your opponent's playing style and/or tactics if you have learned about them through other players or the media. This

will give you an even greater advantage as you con-
front him or her on a hand-to-hand basis.

When You Learn in Advance Which Pro
You Will Play, Study Up on That Person
and It Could Be Your Day

For many players, the first time they learn they'll be facing a pro
is when they *are* facing a pro; in other words, they find out when
they show up at the table ready to play. There's no warning, no
extra time to prepare for the confrontation. All you can do in
cases like these is go with what you already know about the professional, play your A game, and hope for the best.

Then there are the *other* times. These are the situations in
which you learn beforehand the name of a poker star you'll be
facing at the tables. Here are some circumstances where this
might occur: (a) at a tournament where players and tables are
announced in advance; (b) during multiday tournaments where,
at the end of each day, a list is posted that discloses player and
table assignments for the following day; and (c) in cash games
where certain professionals regularly play.

If you should be fortunate enough to have some lead time
before you have to sit down and play a specific professional, use
those hours (or days) to study up on your opponent. If your opponent is a ranked professional who has (a) appeared on television, (b) written any articles and/or books on his or her
strategy, and/or (c) had his or her play analyzed in print, on the
Internet, or in a film, you need to watch and read all you can
from these resources.

Televised tournament appearances are particularly useful

as you prepare to face your opponent. Use these TV tapes like a football coach uses game films of opposing teams: probe for weaknesses, playing patterns, tells—anything that will give you a better handle on how your opponent behaves at the table, and how you can beat him or her. Because the player's hole cards are exposed, you will have a far easier time in deciphering his or her tells and playing strategy than if you were simply watching him or her play "from the rail" in a casino setting.

The great advantage for the reader of this book is you now have a guide to use when studying players on television. Using what you have learned in these chapters, you can decode the behavior of any number of players, looking for specific tells they might have, that will help you when you face them across the table. I can assure you the tells are there. As I mentioned earlier, *every* professional I have studied on television has exhibited at least one tell that could have made me money had I been playing them in a real tournament or ring game.

I have already heard a number of top professionals complaining about the problems they have encountered because of television exposure, particularly those who have made frequent appearances on the air. They know it is difficult to disguise their strategy, and keep their tells undiscovered, when they are playing with their cards exposed. Their behavior can be studied over and over by anyone with a video recorder who knows how to pause, rewind, and replay a videotape.

The professional player's televised exposure is your window of opportunity to see into his or her game, his or her strategy, and tells. Don't pass up this chance to enhance your winning possibilities should you ever receive advance notification that you'll be mixing it up with a poker professional sometime in the foreseeable future.

Enjoy the Memory . . . but Not at All Costs!

At the second Camp Hellmuth, there was a young player who had worked a long time to save up enough money to pay his registration fee. He was excited to be there, and during the camp tournament he ended up at a table with one of the major poker stars. He had been playing a solid game up to that moment, and then he fell apart. When I asked him what happened, he replied, "I panicked and started doing stupid things. I guess I just wasn't ready to play against a champion."

His behavior is understandable. There is a definite "wow" factor when you come face to face with someone like T. J. Cloutier or John Bonetti. It can be exhilarating and intimidating at the same time, and, if you're not careful, a fast exercise in chip extermination!

Frankly, I hope you get a chance to play at a table with a poker champion; I'm sure it's a memory you'll cherish. But don't end up paying too much for that moment. Remember what I've suggested in this chapter. Learn as much as you can about your opponent. Recall that you have an advantage because you are an unknown, and therefore unpredictable. Recognize that the aura of celebrity can have an impact, but that you can counter that impact by having confidence in your knowledge of the game and establishing your own territory at the table. Don't cower in the presence of a poker star! Sit up straight, carry yourself with confidence, and you'll find yourself fitting right in. Avoid eye contact with the celebrity player. Concentrate on the basics, and remember that rookies have gone on to win final tables against the biggest names in the poker world.

So play your game! Don't be intimidated or so starry-eyed that you forget how to read the cards and the people around you.

And about those people around you: don't forget that it is far more likely that one of them, not the poker star, will be responsible for your demise at the table. So be mindful that you have eight adversaries who oppose you, not just one. Now get out there and play like a winner; that way, you'll feel like one regardless of how things turn out.

Chapter 15

For Whom the Tells Toll

In 1963, they tolled for three men on the streets of Cleveland, Ohio. On that fateful date, 39-year veteran Detective Martin McFadden watched two men walk back and forth in front of a store window. They took turns peeking into the shop and walked away. After multiple passes, the two men huddled at the end of the street looking over their shoulders as they spoke to a third person. Concerned that the men were casing the business and intending to rob the store, the detective moved in, patted down one of the men, and found a concealed handgun. The detective arrested the three men, thus thwarting a robbery and averting potential loss of life.

Officer McFadden's detailed observations became the basis for a landmark U.S. Supreme Court decision (*Terry v. Ohio,* 1968, 392 U.S. 1). Since 1968, this ruling has allowed police officers to stop and frisk individuals without a warrant when their behaviors telegraph their intention to commit a crime. With this decision, the Supreme Court acknowledged that nonverbal behaviors presage criminality if those behaviors are properly observed and decoded. Once again, we see a demonstration of the relationship between our thoughts, intentions, and nonverbal behavior. And, most crucial, we have legal recognition that such a relationship exists and is valid.

Holding Court at the Poker Table

Just having a gut feeling or a sense that somebody is up to no good (trying to rob you blind or steal your blind) isn't sufficient proof for the Supreme Court, and it shouldn't be any different for poker players, either. One has to be able to articulate with clarity what is observed, and the significance of that observation, before one is allowed to act. Today, we can do that. Research from the past two decades has permitted us to validate linkages between our thoughts and our actions. In the *Terry v. Ohio* case, careful observation was conducted, behaviors were clearly articulated, and the officer at the scene meticulously defined what each behavior meant. This is no different from you carefully observing an opponent at the poker table, identifying a specific behavior—an opponent suddenly getting her feet in the "ready" position—and then defining what it means: an *intention cue* to take some action.

When it comes to the study of poker tells, we have evolved from the realm of personal experience to professional science. As we learn more about the brain and behavior, we expand our ability to accurately identify and decipher nonverbal behaviors, which, in turn, allows us to assess with increasing certainty what a person intends to do, and the overall honesty of his actions.

Read People Well, and It Will Be Your Opponent for Whom the Tells Toll

OK. You've read the book, you've learned the material, you're wearing your favorite poker shirt, and you're ready to play some cards! Now what?

Now it's time to go forth and play with confidence. Recognize that you now possess a tremendous advantage at the poker table. You have the most up-to-date tools, the most up-to-date knowledge, and the most current scientific strategy for playing winning poker using nonverbal behavior. You have been introduced to the observational skills and scientifically validated tells you will need to read people successfully while concealing your own behavior.

There is nothing to keep you from becoming a better observer and decoder of the world. In a short period of time, as many students have already demonstrated, you will reap the benefits of utilizing these newfound skills. It's time to go out there and have fun putting this new knowledge to work in the cardrooms of your choice. Let this book be your guide as you continue to mature as a player in the days and years to come.

And there's a bonus. The sooner you begin using your newfound knowledge, the more success you will experience. This is because fewer people will have read this book and had time to develop countermeasures. There will always be some players you can count on to be a valuable revenue stream for you: they include those individuals who will never read this book; those who read the book but don't make an effective effort to translate their knowledge into action; and, finally, those who use the book's tactics but then revert to their old ways because they'd rather "play for fun and not have to take the game so seriously." These individuals will provide a constant source of nourishment on the poker food chain for as long as they continue to play.

A Final Thought

Reading people successfully—learning, decoding, and utilizing nonverbal behavior to predict human actions—is a task well worth your time, one that offers ample rewards for the efforts expended. Effective people-reading skills can improve your quality of life whenever and wherever you interact with others. It can make you a winner in that contest we call life. So plant your feet firmly on the floor, keep an eye out for those all-important tells, and get yourself into the game.

Read 'em and reap!

Some Final Thoughts From Phil

You have now read a book that can do nothing but help you at the poker table, particularly if you are an amateur. That is because you will be playing against other amateurs who don't know how to cover themselves up and don't know what tells to look for. They simply don't know the important tells that Joe presents in this book, tells that I've found to be incredibly accurate. What's more, they probably won't take the time to learn them anytime soon, if ever.

What about professionals and would-be professionals? Joe's book will be required reading for every serious player because of the great information he presents. I can guarantee you all the pros are going to rush out to buy this book because they recognize that knowing what he has to say can make them money and not knowing what he has to say can do serious damage to their bankrolls. Joe's reputation in the poker world is already established and wherever he appears, poker players take their time and money and gladly offer it for his advice and playing strategies. Joe's insights have forever changed the landscape of poker, and if you aren't familiar with the new terrain, you simply won't find your way to a profitable destination.

Further, what you learn from *Read 'Em and Reap* has broader applications beyond the poker table. By focusing on the tells described in this book, I have saved a fortune and made a fortune by accurately "reading" people in business. When people come to me with business propositions, I use tells to determine if these individuals feel their proposition is "strong" or "weak," whether it is reasonable or exaggerated. Tells allow me to assess whether the person offering the deal is trustworthy, dedicated, and willing to work on the project, or devious, dishonest, and lazy to a fault. I can "tell" if he or she truly believes in the project. So can you.

Using tells can also be very helpful when dealing with interpersonal relationships. When a career FBI agent has revealed to you nonverbal behaviors he uses to trip up master spies, it is highly probable you will be able to use these same methods to determine when your friend, spouse, or child is lying or telling the truth.

Go out and use the information you have learned in this book. Use it at the card table, the business table, and the dinner table. I am convinced you'll experience a significant difference in the levels of success you achieve; I'm betting you'll be able to "tell" the difference!

Selected Bibliography

Birdwhistell, Ray L. 1971. *Kinesics and Context: Essays on Body-Motion Communication*. Philadelphia: Penguin.

Buck, R. 1994. *The Communication of Emotion*. New York: Guilford Press.

Burgoon, Judee K., David B. Buller, and W. Gill Woodall. 1994. *Nonverbal Communication: The Unspoken Dialogue*. Columbus, Ohio: Greyden Press.

Canter, David, and Laurence Alison. 1998. *Interviewing and Deception*. Dartmouth, England: Ashgate.

Carter, Rita. 1998. *Mapping the Mind*. Los Angeles: University of California Press.

Cialdini, Robert B. 1993. *Influence: The Psychology of Persuasion*. New York: William Morrow.

Clark, Sherrie, and Alan Mock. "Tampa Bay's Spycatcher." *Imago* 4, no. 4 (2004): 16–21.

Collett, Peter. 2003. *The Book of Tells: From the Bedroom to the Boardroom—How to Read Other People.* Ontario: HarperCollins.

Davis, Ann, Joseph Pereira, and William Bulkeley. "Security Concerns Bring Focus on Translating Body Language." *Wall Street Journal,* August 15, 2002.

De Becker, Gavin. 1997. *The Gift of Fear.* New York: Dell.

Dimitrius, Jo-Ellan, and Mark Mazzarela. 2002. *Put Your Best Foot Forward: Make a Great Impression by Taking Control of How Others See You.* New York: Fireside.

———. 1998. *Reading People.* New York: Ballantine.

Duke, Annie. "Annie vs. the FBI." *Bluff,* April–May 2005, 20.

Ekman, Paul. 2003. *Emotions Revealed: Recognizing Faces and Feelings to Improve Communication and Emotional Life.* New York: Times Books.

———. 1985. *Telling Lies: Clues to Deceit in the Marketplace, Politics, and Marriages.* New York: W.W. Norton.

Feldman, Andrew. "Navarro Steals the Show at CH2." ESPN. com, February 24, 2006.

Ford, Charles V. 1996. *Lies! Lies! Lies! The Psychology of Deceit.* Washington, D.C.: American Psychiatric Press.

Givens, David G. 1998–2000. *The Nonverbal Dictionary of Gestures, Signs and Body Language Cues.* Spokane: Center for Nonverbal Studies (http://members.aol.com/nonverbal2/diction1.htm).

Goleman, Daniel. 1995. *Emotional Intelligence.* New York: Bantam.

Guerrero, Laura K., Joseph A. DeVito, and Michael L. Hecht, eds. 1999. *The Nonverbal Communication Reader: Classic and Contemporary Readings,* 2nd ed. Long Grove, Ill.: Waveland Press.

Hall, Edward T. 1959. *The Silent Language*. New York: Doubleday.

Harper, Robert G., Arthur N. Wiens, and Joseph D. Matarazzo. 1978. *Non-Verbal Communications: The State of the Art*. New York: John Wiley & Sons.

Harrison, Randall P. 1974. *Beyond Words: An Introduction to Nonverbal Communication*. Englewood Cliffs, N.J.: Prentice-Hall.

Hellmuth, Phil. 2006. "A Happy Outcome at Camp Hellmuth." *Card Player* 19, no. 7.

Jackiewicz, Dr. Joyce. 2006. Interviewed by Joe Navarro. April 10.

Knapp, Mark L., and Judith A. Hall. 2002. *Nonverbal Communication in Human Interaction*, 5th ed. New York: Harcourt Brace Jovanovich.

LeDoux, Joseph E. 1996. *The Emotional Brain: The Mysterious Underpinnings of Emotional Life*. New York: Touchstone.

MacLean, Paul. 1990. *The Triune Brain in Evolution: Role in Paleocerebral Functions*. New York: Plenum.

Morris, Desmond. 1994. *Bodytalk: The Meaning of Human Gestures*. New York: Crown.

———. 1985. *Body Watching*. New York: Crown.

———. 1980. *Man Watching*. New York: Crown.

———. 1977. *Manwatching: A Field Guide to Human Behavior*. New York: Harry N. Abrams.

———. 1971. *Intimate Behavior*. New York: Random House.

Morris, Desmond, et al. 1994. *Gestures*. New York: Scarborough.

Morrison, Terri, Wayne A. Conaway, and George A. Borden. 1994. *Kiss Bow, or Shake Hands: How to Do Business in*

Sixty Countries. Holbrook, Mass.: Adams Media Corporation.

Murphy, Dave. "Reading Body Language Can Help Unmask a Bluffer." *San Francisco Chronicle,* September 24, 2005.

Navarro, Joe. 2006. Interview. *Bluff,* January 2006, 40–41.

———. 2005. "Your Stage Presence: Nonverbal Communication." In *Successful Trial Strategies for Prosecutors,* ed. Candace M. Mosley, 13–19. Columbia, S.C.: National College of District Attorneys.

———. 2004. "Testifying in the Theater of the Courtroom." *FBI Law Enforcement Bulletin* (September): 26–30.

———. 2003. "A Four Domain Model of Detecting Deception." *FBI Law Enforcement Bulletin* (June): 19–24.

Navarro, Joe, and John R. Schafer. 2003. "Universal Principles of Criminal Behavior: A Tool for Analyzing Criminal Intent. *FBI Law Enforcement Bulletin* (January): 22–24.

———. 2001. "Detecting Deception." *FBI Law Enforcement Bulletin* (July): 9–13.

Schafer, John R., and Joe Navarro. 2004. *Advanced Interviewing Techniques.* Springfield, Ill.: Charles C. Thomas.

Steere, David A. 1982. *Bodily Expressions in Psychotherapy.* New York: Brunner/Mazel.

Vrij, Aldert. 2000. *Detecting Lies and Deceit: The Psychology of Lying and the Implications for Professional Practice.* Chichester, England: John Wiley & Sons.

Vrij, Aldert, and G.R. Semin. 1996. "Lie Experts' Beliefs about Nonverbal Indicators of Deception." *Journal of Nonverbal Behavior* 20: 65–80.

Vrij, Aldert, Katherine Edward, Kim P. Roberts, and Ray Bull. 2000. "Detecting Deception via Analysis of Verbal and

Nonverbal Behavior." *Journal of Nonverbal Behavior* 24, no. 4 (Winter 2000): 239–263.

Zunin, L., and Zunin, N. 1972. *Contact—The First Four Minutes.* New York: Ballantine.

Index